Strategic Restructuring for Nonprofit Organizations

Mergers, Integrations, and Alliances

AMELIA KOHM AND
DAVID LA PIANA

D0068752

PRAEGER

Westport, Connecticut
London

Library of Congress Cataloging-in-Publication Data

Kohm, Amelia, 1967–
    Strategic restructuring for nonprofit organizations : mergers, integrations, and alliances /
Amelia Kohm and David La Piana.
        p. cm.
    Includes bibliographical references and index.
    ISBN 0–275–98069–3 (alk. paper)
        1. Nonprofit organizations—United States—Management.   2. Corporate
    reorganizations—United States.   3. Consolidation and merger of corporations—United
    States.   4. Strategic alliances (Business)—United States.   I. La Piana, David, 1954–
    II. Title.
    HD62.6.K64 2003
    658.1′6—dc22   2003058000

British Library Cataloguing in Publication Data is available.

Library of Congress Catalog Card Number: 2003058000
ISBN: 0–275–98069–3

First published in 2003

Praeger Publishers, 88 Post Road West, Westport, CT 06881
An imprint of Greenwood Publishing Group, Inc.
www.praeger.com

Printed in the United States of America

The paper used in this book complies with the
Permanent Paper Standard issued by the National
Information Standards Organization (Z39.48–1984).

10 9 8 7 6 5 4 3 2 1

Strategic Restructuring for Nonprofit Organizations

For Geoff, with love

For Mary, Marisa and Tessa, with love

Contents

Figure and Tables   ix

Acknowledgments   xi

1   The Rules (and Conditions) of the Game Are Changing   1

2   Fundamental Questions   11

3   How Prevalent Are Strategic Restructuring Partnerships?   17

4   What Is Driving the Formation of Strategic Restructuring
    Partnerships?   23

5   What Are the Benefits of Strategic Restructuring
    Partnerships?   31

6   What Are the Costs and Challenges of Strategic
    Restructuring Partnerships?   39

7   What Factors Contribute to Successful Strategic
    Restructuring Partnerships?   55

8   The Future Impact of Strategic Restructuring on the
    Nonprofit Sector   61

9   Conclusion   69

Appendix A: Case Study Stories   79

Appendix B: Methodology (Overview)   119

Appendix C: Methodology and Findings from Prevalence Survey   123

Appendix D: Telephone Survey Form   131

Appendix E: Study Participants   133

Appendix F: Case Study Partnerships   141

Bibliography   143

Index   147

Figure and Tables

Figure 1.1   Partnership Matrix   5

Table 9.1   Common Benefits and Costs and Challenges of
             Strategic Restructuring by Type of Partnership   70

Table A.1   Joint Programming Partnership   80

Table A.2   Administrative Consolidation Partnership   83

Table A.3   Management Service Organization Partnership   90

Table A.4   Partners for Community Affiliates   94

Table A.5   Joint Venture Partnership   97

Table A.6   Parent-Subsidiary Partnership   103

Table A.7   Merger   112

Table C.1   Overall Survey Yield   124

Table C.2   Cleveland Survey Yield   125

Table C.3   San Francisco Survey Yield   126

Table C.4   Strategic Restructuring Experience by Total
             Revenues   126

Table C.5   Strategic Restructuring Experience by Total
             Revenues   126

Table C.6   Motivations for Forming Strategic Restructuring
            Partnerships   128

Table C.7   Benefits of Strategic Restructuring Partnerships   129

Acknowledgments

We would like to thank the organizations that opened their doors to us and let us interview their staff, board members, and funders: ACHIEVE, Core Behavioral Health Care, Every Woman's House, Inc., Kentucky Art and Craft Foundation, Louisville Visual Art Association, Northwest Business Development Association, Partners for Community, Speed Art Museum, Spokane County Microenterprise Development Program, Spokane Neighborhood Action Program, STEPS (Substance Abuse, Treatment, Education, and Prevention Services) at Liberty Center, Inc., and Talbert House. We also extend our gratitude to the 20 nonprofit sector leaders and the 262 representatives of nonprofits in San Francisco and Cleveland who participated in telephone interviews. Without the time and consideration they volunteered, our research would not have been possible.

Of course, we are also indebted to the foundations that contributed support to Phase I and Phase II of the study: Surdna Foundation, the Lilly Endowment, the George Gund Foundation, the Nonprofit Sector Research Fund of the Aspen Institute, the William and Flora Hewlett Foundation, the James Irvine Foundation, and the David and Lucile Packard Foundation. Thank you for recognizing the need for research in this area.

Thank you to our study advisory committee that included:

Jay C. Bloom
President and CEO
Morrison Center Child and Family Services in Portland Oregon

David Campbell
Vice President, Policy and Program
Community Service Society of New York

James E. Canales
Vice President
The James Irvine Foundation

Marcia Egbert
Senior Program Officer
The George Gund Foundation

Renu Karir
Program Associate
The William and Flora Hewlett Foundation

Charles F. Logie Jr.
Vice President, Support Services
Arbor Circle

Thomas McLaughlin
BDO Seidman LLP

Avis C. Vidal
Principal Senior Associate
The Urban Institute

Diane Vinokur-Kaplan
Professor
University of Michigan

We were also aided by Stephen Baker, Diana Mendley Rauner, and Joan Wynn, who served on a study advisory committee at Chapin Hall Center for Children.

Finally, very special thanks to some key individuals who provided much advice, many reviews, and occasional emotional support along the way: Heather Gowdy, Harold Richman, Joan Costello, LaShanda Ticer-Wurr, and Anne Clary.

CHAPTER 1

The Rules (and Conditions) of the Game Are Changing

There was a time when starting and growing a nonprofit organization was a relatively simple matter. Someone was worried about pregnant teenagers. She found others who shared her concern and filled out some forms from the state and the Internal Revenue Service (IRS). With an office or maybe just a room in a church basement, she was in business. Perhaps revenues were low, but with volunteer labor and donated space, so were expenses.

What she probably didn't give much thought to was anything like market analysis. Nor did she speak with anyone like a banker or venture capitalist. She could raise capital by collecting donations from friends and colleagues without offering up any hard numbers about need or demand for the services or resources she planned to offer (especially at this early stage). And because the recipients of her organization's services and those paying the bills were not necessarily the same people—a condition economists call *contract failure*—she could persist despite a lack of information about the quality and effectiveness of the organization's work. This isn't to say that contract failure inevitably leads to inefficiency. Certainly many nonprofits offer valuable services that would not be possible without the generosity of individual donors, foundations, and corporations. (In this situation, these questions probably never even occurred to the founder.)

Take a real life example. Talbert House was born when a group of citizens in Cincinnati, Ohio met to talk about helping men recently released from prison. They raised $10,000 from private donations and set up a small halfway house. Talbert had its first growth spurt when it received a government grant in 1966. Several more leaps followed in the 1970s and

1980s, and Talbert gradually expanded the scope of its services to include mental health, substance abuse treatment, and employment programs. It also added women and adolescents to the client base.

Grants—particularly government grants—come with requirements and regulations. To fulfill these obligations, organizations often must have certain management structures, financial systems, and client-tracking procedures. So the organization became more structured and hierarchical over the years. Today, Talbert House is a citywide, multiservice organization with a budget exceeding $25 million.[1]

For some organizations in the nonprofit sector—which includes not just human services but also religious, educational, environmental, cultural, and civic-improvement organizations—the scenario has not changed much over the past forty years. But for many, like Talbert House, the funding environment has changed so significantly that they are rethinking the basic structures of their operations.

So, what has changed?

- The number of nonprofit organizations in the United States more than doubled between 1982 and 1997, creating a more competitive market for grants and donations in some parts of the sector. This is particularly relevant to government grants, which have remained stagnant or decreased in many funding areas in recent years (2001).[2]

- For-profits have entered into markets traditionally dominated by nonprofits, such as health care and childcare, heightening competition.

- With the advent of managed care strategies and block grants, the federal, state, and local governments have transformed themselves into purchasers of outcomes rather than buyers of services.[3] A survey of 45 states found that 25 were delivering mental health and/or substance abuse service via managed care. Such contracting structures are meant to spur greater efficiency and integration among social service organizations (1999).[4]

- Many private and public funders are looking for more hard evidence of "return on investment." To respond to this concern, some nonprofits need more sophisticated client-tracking and evaluation strategies, which often require technology too expensive for a single community-based organization to develop or purchase on its own.

- Keeping experienced, talented leaders has grown more difficult. A survey of more than 1,000 nonprofit executives in four U.S. cities found that most executives have been in their positions fewer than five years and have never previously headed a nonprofit. Moreover, fewer than half intend to take another top job at a nonprofit when they leave their current position (Peters & Wolfred, 2001).

What do these changes mean? How will they affect the decisions nonprofits make about their futures?

Some nonprofits will respond to these and similar changes in traditional ways, resulting in relatively minor shifts in the way their organizations work. For example, some managers may decide that stiffer competition calls for increased stringency. They may pare down administrative staff, close programs that are not popular with funders, or focus exclusively on program areas neglected by other organizations, where they hope they will not have to compete for funds.

Others may conclude that, although statistics like those listed are indeed dramatic, the implications for their particular organizations are not clear. They have heard dire predictions before and lived through them. They will carry on business as usual, perhaps making some incremental changes along the way.

Still others will take more dramatic steps, altering their organizations' philosophies and structures. Organizational leaders who believe that changing times call for new approaches may look for new sources of money. They may decide to begin charging clients for previously free services or to increase existing client fees. Some may consider starting a business (e.g., catering, T-shirt sales, printing and copying), hoping to generate revenues to support their primary mission (e.g., helping teen parents, protecting forests, providing access to great art).

Some nonprofits may think about how they can combine their resources and expertise with that of other organizations to realize some economies of scale and perhaps to position themselves to win more government grants and contracts. Several years ago, Talbert House chose to take this step. (For more on how Talbert House formed a parent-subsidiary relationship with a mental health organization, see the discussion later in this volume.)

This book is for nonprofit managers, board members, funders, consultants, and others who want to know more about this last option—an option we call *strategic restructuring.* Strategic restructuring includes both partial and full consolidations among nonprofit organizations, and thus it refers to a range of partnership options, from those that involve joint programs or shared administrative functions to full-scale mergers.

The only reference points for many nonprofits considering strategic restructuring are large corporate mergers, which differ in significant ways from nonprofit mergers and shed no light at all on partial consolidations. Little writing and even less research on nonprofit consolidations exists. Although some consultants and funders have proclaimed that strategic restructuring (or another term referring to the same group of strategies) is or will be a wave overtaking the sector, reliable information on the macro and micro impact of strategic restructuring is in short supply.

Strategic restructuring appears to be following the course of many new (or refurbished) management strategies, from total quality management to zero-based budgeting. The existence of the trend, the value of the strategy, and the attendant best practices become truisms long before any research substantiates these claims. Managers thus make changes based on ideology and anecdotes.

This book is based on information we have gathered through conversations with many managers, staff, and board members who have engaged in strategic restructuring. Our research helps answer questions about the impact of strategic restructuring on individual organizations, questions such as

- What are the benefits of strategic restructuring to various types of nonprofits? To whom do the benefits accrue, and to what degree?
- What are the costs and challenges of strategic restructuring? Who bears the greatest burden of these costs?
- Under what circumstances do the costs outweigh the benefits, and vice versa?

We also explore the current and potential impact of strategic restructuring on the nonprofit sector as a whole by addressing such questions as

- How prevalent are strategic restructuring partnerships in the nonprofit sector today?
- Will such partnerships increase? What do leaders in the sector expect in this regard?
- If such partnerships do increase, what may be the implications for the sector?

Our answers are based on a three-year study on the topic—including surveys of over 400 nonprofits nationwide, six in-depth case studies, and interviews of 20 leaders in the nonprofit sector. (For more on the research, see Appendix B.)

WHAT IS STRATEGIC RESTRUCTURING?

When we started studying strategic restructuring in 1999, we knew that nonprofits were merging for a variety of reasons and that they were also trying some interesting partial consolidations—partnerships in which nonprofits shared staff members or buildings, or jointly operated programs. However, there was no research on the range of partnerships that existed and no data on how common they were. Indeed, when we spoke to staff at organizations that had tried partial consolidations, they often told us that they knew of no other similar partnerships.

So our first step was to map the terrain, to determine what types of partnerships existed. We then looked at how prevalent they were and at what we could learn from people who had tried (successfully or not) strategic restructuring.

We surveyed 192 strategic restructuring partnerships from around the United States, and, from the information they provided, we identified six types of partnerships that fall into two major categories: those that involve some change in corporate structure, including the creation or dissolution of an organization—we called these *integrations*,—and those that involve the sharing of programs, staff, facilities, and/or equipment but require no changes to organizational structure—we called these *alliances*.

The Partnership Matrix (see Figure 1.1) shows that partnerships are primarily distinguished by whether they focus on programmatic functions (such as counseling, curatorial duties, advocacy) or on administrative functions (accounting, fundraising, human resources, managing facilities). Partnerships that involve both functions are placed in the middle part of

Figure 1.1
Partnership Matrix

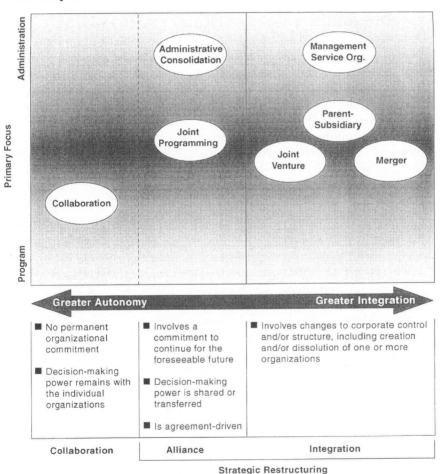

the matrix. Partnerships that involve few integrated functions are closer to the left side of the matrix, and those that involve greater consolidation are toward the right.

Please note that we have included on the matrix one type of partnership that is *not* strategic restructuring—collaboration. Collaboration is variously defined by different people in different situations. We use it to refer to organizational partnerships that are about sharing information or coordinating efforts but do not include shared, transferred, or combined services, resources, or programs. Collaboration thus sits on the far left side of the matrix to indicate that there is no integration among the participating organizations. Additionally, because programs, rather than administrative functions, are most often the focus of collaboration, collaboration appears near the bottom of the matrix.

Alliances

The two types of alliances on the matrix are joint programming and administrative consolidation. Both are agreement-driven, meaning that the organizations commit, usually in writing, to an ongoing partnership. These alliances also involve joint management of one or more organizational functions. In a joint-programming situation, one or more programs are jointly managed; with administrative consolidations, one or more back-office (administrative) functions are shared. Beyond the joint efforts, however, the partners operate independently. Following are brief examples of each of these types of partnerships from our case studies. The stories of these cases appear throughout the book.

Joint Programming

Spokane Neighborhood Action Program, a human service organization offering a wide range of programs for low-income residents of Spokane, Washington, formed a micro-enterprise program with Northwest Business Development Association, which provides loans to small businesses in the Spokane area. The two organizations jointly run the program, which recruits, educates, and provides loans to low-income adults interested in starting small businesses. Outside of the micro-enterprise program, the two organizations function independently.

Administrative Consolidation

STEPS (Substance Abuse, Treatment, Education, and Prevention Services) at Liberty Center, Inc., and Every Woman's House, a shelter for abused women, conducted a joint capital campaign and now jointly own the building that houses their offices in Wooster, Ohio. The two organizations also share some office equipment and several administrative staff, including an executive director. Their programs, however, operate independently, under the governance of separate boards of directors.

Integrations

The four types of integrations on the Partnership Matrix are management service organization (MSO), joint venture, parent-subsidiary, and merger. These partnerships share the characteristics of alliances but also involve changes to corporate control or structure, including the creation or dissolution of one or more organizations.

MSOs are organizations that nonprofits establish to provide some or all of their back-office functions for them. Joint ventures involve two or more organizations creating a new organization to further a specific administrative or programmatic end. In a parent-subsidiary, one organization oversees another. Although the visibility and identity of the original independent organizations often remain intact in a parent-subsidiary relationship, some organizations involved in such restructurings consolidate to the point where they look and function much like a single merged organization. Finally, through mergers, previously separate organizations completely combine programmatic and administrative functions as well as governance. Sometimes this involves the creation of a new nonprofit corporation, and sometimes one or more organizations dissolve and become part of another.

Following are brief examples of each of these types of partnerships from our case studies. The full story of each appears later in the book.

Management Service Organization (MSO)

Corporation for Public Management and New England Farm Workers' Council, both multipurpose human service organizations serving Springfield, Massachusetts, and the surrounding area, established a new organization, Partners for Community (PfC), to provide all of the back-office functions for their agencies. PfC also provides more limited administrative support to four smaller organizations that are affiliates of the MSO.

Joint Venture

Speed Art Museum, Kentucky Art and Craft Foundation, and Louisville Visual Art Association, the three major visual arts organizations in Louisville, Kentucky, created a limited liability company to jointly operate a gift store and gallery.

Parent-Subsidiary

Talbert House, a multipurpose human service organization in Cincinnati, Ohio, became the parent of Core Behavioral Health Care, a mental health agency. Through the partnership, the organizations have consolidated all of their administrative functions, their policies and procedures, and some of their programs. Core pays Talbert a management fee for administrative services. Talbert's board appoints Core's board, and three Core members sit on Talbert's board. Core's executive director reports to Talbert's, but the Core board retains significant input to hire and fire its leader.

Merger

Zonta Services and Peninsula Children's Center, two agencies that provided educational, mental health, and other services to children with physical and mental disabilities in the San Francisco Bay area, dissolved their organizations and merged all of their functions to become a new agency called ACHIEVE.

HOW THIS BOOK IS ORGANIZED

Chapter 2 poses some fundamental questions about the nonprofit sector. How one answers them informs how one views strategic restructuring. These questions concern the nature and effect of competition in the nonprofit sector, the characteristics that help organizations to win financial support, and whether nonprofits tend to be "bloated" or "anorexic" when it comes to administrative resources. This chapter may be of particular interest to funders, consultants, association heads, and others whose decisions affect a broad range of organizations.

In chapters 3 through 8, we address the following questions by drawing on the findings from our study and related research

- How prevalent are strategic restructuring partnerships?
- What is driving the formation of different strategic restructuring partnerships?
- What are the benefits of strategic restructuring to partner organizations?
- What are the costs and challenges of strategic restructuring?
- What are some of the factors contributing to the success of various types of partnerships?
- From the evidence gathered, what appear to be the effects of strategic restructuring partnerships on the nonprofit sector as a whole? What might be the future impact of such partnerships?

We use actual cases to illustrate how particular organizations first became involved in strategic restructuring partnerships, how they planned and implemented these partnerships, the current status of these partnerships, and the organizations' future plans and directions. Not all cases are success stories. Rather, they are real-world examples of the costs and benefits of strategic restructuring. As such, they will be useful to anyone con-templating forming or supporting such a partnership.

Please note that the descriptions of the case study partnerships included in the book are snapshots in time. We collected information from the or-ganizations during the winter and spring of 2001. Since that time, all of the organizations have experienced changes in their partnerships, their staffs, and other aspects of their operations. These changes are not noted in the text.

The book ends with a summary of our conclusions based upon our research and that of others, as well as recommendations for further re-search. The appendices include a description of the research methodology, a description of the prevalence survey we conducted and its results, a copy of the telephone survey form that we used, a list of those who par-ticipated in the study, and a bibliography.

We hope the experiences and learning of those who have lived through various types of nonprofit consolidations will help you make better de-cisions about strategic restructuring. We look forward to your feedback.

NOTES

1. The story is not always this simple or rosy. Some nonprofits falter. But many of those significantly reduce their operations (until, for example, the only remnant of an organization is a volunteer sending letters from his or her kitchen table) or never get around to notifying their attorney general or IRS that they are no longer operating. This phenomenon makes it difficult to know how many nonprofits thrive rather than simply, at least in name, survive.

2. The Nonprofit Almanac published by The Independent Sector in Washing-ton, D.C. in 2001

3. Managed care refers to a range of approaches employed by insurance com-panies or government agencies to balance the cost of services with quality and access. Such approaches include pre-authorization for care, built-in financial risks and incentives for care providers, and outcome-based contracting. When govern-ment agencies employ managed care strategies in their contracting with human services, they tend to favor larger organizations that can provide a variety of services at relatively lower costs due to economies of scale.

4. The State Mental Health Agency Profiling System on the Web site of The National Association of State Mental Health Program Directors Research Institute, Inc. <nri.rdmc.org> 2001.

CHAPTER 2

Fundamental Questions

A few fundamental questions lurk behind almost every other question about strategic restructuring. These questions concern the nature and effect of competition in the nonprofit sector, the characteristics that help organizations to win financial support, and whether nonprofits tend to be "bloated" or "anorexic" when it comes to administrative resources.[1] The answers to these questions vary according to the viewpoint of the questioner. It is important to keep in mind both the questions and the perspectives they evoke, when considering strategic restructuring.

HOW SHOULD COMPETITION WORK IN THE NONPROFIT SECTOR?

"Calls for improved coordination are . . . heard from the left, right, and center and have come to resemble a mantra that, if repeated often enough, will obliterate lacking coherence in human services" (Reitan, 1998).

Few people these days are challenging the conventional wisdom that nonprofits, particularly human service organizations, unnecessarily replicate one another's services. By the term "unnecessary replication" we do not mean that there is too much of a particular service—in fact, the opposite argument could be made in many fields. For example, most communities have a dearth of quality childcare, and waiting lists are common for counseling, drug rehabilitation, and other social services. Rather, many funders and others who deal with nonprofits feel there are too many *organizations* offering similar services, each organization requiring overhead such as facilities, administrative staff, and equipment. According to this line of thinking, a smaller number of larger agencies could offer services more efficiently. Indeed, by saving administrative dollars, they might be able to offer more services.

This concern is not confined to the human service sector. In one of the earliest articles on strategic restructuring, a manager of an arts organization is quoted as saying, "It seems ridiculous that if you have a dozen organizations, each producing a small number of events every year, you also have a dozen executive directors, a dozen office leases, a dozen marketing departments. None of the organizations can really afford to engage as much staff as it needs" (Scheff & Kotler, 1996). The logic seems indisputable. However, it remains unclear if such replication is indeed "ridiculous," and, if so, just how ridiculous.

Interestingly, the term "efficiency," when applied to nonprofits, often takes on a different meaning than in a for-profit context. The idea that demand and supply will influence each other and that competition makes the system efficient does not work in many sectors of the nonprofit market. Contract failure—the term economists use to describe situations in which those receiving goods and services are not the same people or institutions as those paying for them—can lead to problems in the regulation of supply and demand in the sector.[2]

Take an everyday example. When we see several gas stations within a five-block radius, most of us do not question whether they are unnecessarily replicating each other's services. We assume that the demand is strong enough to warrant this level of supply. We may also note that, due to their proximity, the stations are competing and thus keeping prices down. If there is an excess of supply, one or more stations will likely close.

By contrast, when we see three similar organizations in one small city providing employment services to homeless adults, concerns regarding redundancy and inefficiency may arise because we have no clear sense of what the demand for these services is. Certainly the interest among funders and donors in these organizations and their services is high enough to keep them alive (although they may not be thriving). But what about homeless adults' interest in and need for these services? Could one larger organization provide more and/or better services than three smaller ones? Or would a larger organization be too bureaucratic and impersonal to respond quickly to its clients' needs? Would one organization provide only one service location and thus be too far away for some of its clients? And would a larger organization limit the types of services available to homeless adults? Just as different gas stations offer different combinations of services (car wash, mechanical service, oil change, etc.), so too do employment organizations (resume development, interviewing skills, job placement services, etc.).

In the for-profit sector, we assume that competition weeds out businesses that perform poorly in terms of the quality of their goods or services, the efficiency of their administration, or their ability to assess consumer demand. However, in many areas of the nonprofit sector—again, particularly human services—it is not clear what strategies work best under what conditions. So many factors affect whether an alcoholic stays sober (family pressure, work situation, and personal resolve, to name just a few) that it is difficult to assess the impact of one substance abuse program. Thus clients may continue to use, and funders continue to support, services that do not work well or at all. Alternatively, they may reject a service that *is* effective but only over the long-term. They often do not have enough information to use in their decision making.

Stephen Wernet, the editor of *Managed Care in Human Services,* concludes that, despite the efforts of managed care programs to direct dollars to the most efficient and effective services,

The historical outcome of cost containment in behavioral health care has been, at best, mixed. It has been notoriously expensive to consume and deliver behavioral health care service. Certainly, less is known about what type of service works effectively with which clinical problem constellation, and therefore, about how much time is necessary for treatment to remedy a given behavioral health problem. (Wernet, 1999)

Simply put, for many organizations, it is just not clear what works. In the words of two sociologists, the connections between "means and ends are obscure or uncertain, [and thus] carefully designed adaptations may have completely unexpected consequences. Moreover, short-run consequences may often differ greatly from long-run consequences" (Hannan & Freeman, 1984).

So the optimal quantity and range of services in the sector and what (if any) role competition may play in pushing the sector toward optimal levels of supply remain unclear. What is apparent, however, is the fact that how we answer these questions will affect our view of strategic restructuring. In the corporate world, businesses buy and sell one another, partner, and launch joint ventures based on clear financial indicators. They may fail due to faulty data or strategy, but they rarely question their model. In the nonprofit sector, we have no model, so the questions raised by strategic restructuring are not anchored in a common view of how the sector should function.

WHAT CHARACTERISTICS HELP ORGANIZATIONS WIN FINANCIAL SUPPORT?

Researchers who study organizations of all types—nonprofit, public, and corporate—have a number of theories about why organizations act the way they do. One theory (called resource dependency theory) says that organizations are mostly concerned about maintaining a predictable income stream, and if you understand this one fact about organizations, you can understand the structures, strategies, and policies they choose. For many nonprofits, the business of maintaining a steady revenue flow is about finding ways to attract and keep funders. Often this means divining the (real or imagined) wishes, concerns, and future decisions of potential contributors.

Given the difficulty in assessing the work of many nonprofits, as previously discussed, how do corporations, foundations, individual donors, and paying clients make decisions about where to invest their resources? A body of research and theoretical work points to the following answer: dollars will flow to organizations that *appear* to be efficient or effective according to the latest thinking on what "efficient" or "effective" is.

Paul DiMaggio and Walter Powell discuss how institutional gatekeepers, such as funders, often regard the use of what they call managerial tactics (e.g., devising strategic plans, aggressively marketing services, and strategic restructuring) as indications of organizational accountability, reliability, and trustworthiness (Galaskiewicz & Bielefeld, 1998). When Joseph Galaskiewicz and Wolfgang Bielefeld studied the reasons behind changes in nonprofits in the Minneapolis–St. Paul metropolitan area from 1980 to 1994, they found that elites (such as funders) increasingly encouraged the use of managerial tactics among the organizations they supported (Galaskiewicz & Bielefeld, 1998). The appearance of such tactics—regardless of their effects—was deemed important. Again, in the absence of a nonprofit business model we look for proxies of efficiency. One need only look to the growing use of the term "CEO" for the nonprofit executive director to see this phenomenon. The change in title often changes nothing internally—it only changes the hoped-for perception of efficiency by the public and particularly by donors and funders.

DiMaggio and Powell contend that, today, changes in organizational structure are less driven by competition or a need for efficiency than by processes that make organizations more similar—processes they call isomorphism. They suggest that in its initial stages an organizational field—comprised of organizations that produce similar services or products—displays diversity, but once the field is established, there is a push toward homogenization. "As an innovation spreads, a threshold is reached beyond which adoption provides legitimacy rather than improves performance" (DiMaggio & Powell, 1983). They point to several causes for institutional isomorphism, including the interests and expectations of funders, organizations' tendency to mimic other organizations perceived as having more legitimacy, and professional networks that advocate for certain structures and approaches.

Is providing "legitimate" services through "legitimate" structures the best way to win support, as DiMaggio and Powell suggest? Or do corporations, foundations, individual donors, and paying clients have enough information to make good decisions about where to put their money? Again, these are questions whose answers will evoke different perspectives on strategic restructuring. For example, those who answer yes to the first question may see the main benefit of strategic restructuring as the opportunity to associate with an organization with a good reputation. In some cases, organizations that subscribe to this belief merge principally to persuade their donors that they are serious about efficiency. Those who answer yes to the latter question, on the other hand, may feel that those paying for nonprofit services are making sound choices, and thus the sector includes the right number and range of organizations.

ARE NONPROFITS BLOATED OR ANOREXIC?

Another open question is whether nonprofits are top-heavy, wasting funds on administration that could be spent on services, or, rather, operating with such skeletal management crews that they do not have enough resources to innovate, grow, or otherwise strengthen their work.

The lack of available information on the efficiency of nonprofit organizations complicates attempts to determine the optimal ratio of administrative to program expenses. Perspectives vary. Does strategic restructuring aggravate organizational anorexia by further paring down management, or does it relieve administrative bloatedness? Some think that consolidation helps to streamline administration, while others feel that it places undue pressure on already stressed managers.

For many nonprofits, such questions appear moot. It is quite clear that they cannot afford an adequate administrative structure. Building this kind of infrastructure would require unacceptable reductions in programming, to the point of bringing into question the organization's viability. Most funders probably would not accept 35 percent, 50 percent, or more of their grants being spent on administration, and managers might find increasing resistance from their front-line staff if they devoted more funds to administration. In such a situation, strategic restructuring may provide (for example, through a merger or an MSO model) a programmatic scale that makes possible a sound management structure. Nonprofits that share basic administrative functions such as an executive director and finance, audit, and human resources management, may find economies of scale in these areas, as in group purchasing of health care or office supplies.

Another important question is how well managed our society expects nonprofits to be. The post–September 11 troubles of major charities reveal some striking management and governance lapses. Many of these nonprofits are among that class of large organizations that can and do spend great sums on management. If these types of institutions are struggling with management issues, can we reasonably expect the neighborhood center with an executive director who also serves as bookkeeper, fundraiser, human resources manager, and snow shoveler, or the childcare center that lacks enough resources to put together financial statements, to be adequately managed? Is there enough public support to spend a larger portion of such institutions' income to become better managed?

With these basic questions about nonprofits in mind, we move now to the answers that we and others have found to questions about strategic restructuring.

NOTES

1. The term "organizational anorexia" was borrowed from Christine Letts, Lecturer in Public Policy; Associate Director, Hauser Center for Nonprofit Institutions, Harvard University.

2. In her study on the financing of Chicago area nonprofit social service and community development organizations, Kirsten Grønbjerg found that only 5 percent of social service organizations and 13 percent of community development organizations receive half or more of their revenues from fees, sales, or dues. Most are dependent on foundations, government agencies, and individual donors for their revenues (Grønbjerg, 1993). Thus the "payer" and the "receiver" of services are different parties.

CHAPTER 3

How Prevalent Are Strategic Restructuring Partnerships?

WHAT OTHERS HAVE FOUND

Many nonprofit experts expect a wave of consolidation among nonprofits, just like the mergers that have swept through corporations over the last decade, as organizations seek the scale necessary for success in the 21st century.... For all its growth, however, the nonprofit sector is highly fragmented, with many organizations too small to accomplish much and many duplicating the works of other organizations. (Johnston, 2000)

Although many executive directors, funders, and others working with nonprofits have heard such proclamations, there is limited research to back up these claims. What research does exist does not provide a clear picture of how many nonprofits are trying strategic restructuring or what types of organizations are most likely to do so. Moreover, current research is often based on small samples, so it's difficult to determine if results pertain to nonprofits in general.

Two surveys of Maryland nonprofits may suggest an increase in strategic restructuring in recent years. One of the studies, conducted in 1999, involved a statewide survey of 439 nonprofits. The other surveyed 325 nonprofits that were members of the Maryland Association of Nonprofits in 1998/1999.[1] Twenty-seven percent of the respondents to the 1995 survey and 58 percent of the respondents to the 1998/1999 survey were sharing resources such as facilities and equipment with other agencies (Salamon, 1997).

A study in 2000 of how welfare reform has affected 90 organizations serving families that qualify for welfare assistance in southeastern Michigan predicted that the rate of resource sharing would be quite high, given that over 75 percent of the respondents reported competition with other agencies for resources and nearly half reported competition for clients. However, the researchers found that only 35 percent had engaged in interorganizational fundraising/resource sharing (Reisch & Sommerfeld, 2000; Reisch & Sommerfeld, 2001).

Some recent studies have found rates of strategic restructuring that are low by any standard. For example, a 1999 survey of 191 nonprofits with operating budgets of $5 million to $50 million in New York City found that respondents ranked partnering and alliance issues low on their priority lists (Abzug & Green, 1999) Whether the size of these organizations' budgets decreased their likelihood of being interested in strategic restructuring is not clear. Other studies, like the Maryland studies and our own, suggest that large organizations may be more apt to consolidate. Clearly, we need more research to better understand the relationship (if any) between an organization's budget size and its chances of trying strategic restructuring.

Other research suggests an increase in strategic restructuring among various types of nonprofits over the last decade. Strategic Solutions, a five-year foundation-funded initiative conducting research on strategic restructuring, looked at the prevalence of articles about mergers or consolidations among nonprofits in local, regional, and national newspapers.[2] This review found that, prior to the mid-1990s, most such articles were about consolidations among hospitals and health care systems. In the last five years, this balance has changed, with many more articles about nonprofits in the arts, human services, community development, environment, and other non–health-related fields.

Recent studies also provide a little information on what types of strategic restructuring partnerships are most common. The Maryland surveys suggest that more organizations are going through partial consolidations (in which only certain programs or operations are shared), as opposed to full-scale consolidations (in which all functions are merged). Four percent of respondents to the 1995 Maryland statewide survey and 6 percent in the 1998/99 Maryland Association of Nonprofits members survey had been through mergers (Salamon, 1997). However, a survey of 198 Arizona nonprofit human service agencies in 1991 found that 27 of the respondents (14 percent) had attempted merger to adapt to funding reductions or unexpected expenses (McMurtry, Netting, & Kettner, 1991).

Although it is difficult to find studies on the prevalence of nonprofit consolidation (much less draw sound conclusions from their findings), a more established body of work suggests that nonprofits often lack the experience or ability to form interorganizational partnerships of any kind.

Collaboration, according to Pennie G. Foster-Fishman, professor of organizational/community psychology at the University of Illinois at Chicago, and her colleagues, is often hampered by funding disincentives, poor communication, organizational rivalries, and service sector segregation (Foster-Fishman, Salem, Allen, & Fahrbach, 1999). In fact, Hillel Schmid, professor of social work at Hebrew University of Jerusalem, maintains that organizations spend most of their time just trying to get by: "research on social service organizations suggests that administrators tend to spend more time in organizational maintenance and control than in such goal-oriented activities as planning, research procurement, innovation, and representation" (Schmid, 1992). Kirsten Grønbjerg, professor of philanthropic studies at the Indiana University Center on Philanthropy, drew a similar conclusion, based on her study of the responsiveness of organizations providing human services to changes in their environments. She found that these organizations often lack the flexibility or organizational culture to make significant changes, and that what organizational change does occur, usually involves only alterations to existing services (Grønbjerg, 1993).

WHAT WE FOUND

To gain a better sense of the prevalence of strategic restructuring, we conducted a survey. We chose a random sample of 400 nonprofits from a pool of 840 human service or cultural organizations with annual revenues of $200,000 or more in San Francisco, California, and Cleveland, Ohio. We surveyed these organizations, primarily by phone, asking several questions regarding key aspects of our definition of strategic restructuring to determine whether the organizations had strategic restructuring experience. (See appendices for more on survey methodology and results.)

Of the 262 organizations that responded to the survey, 62 (24 percent) had some type of strategic restructuring experience. Cleveland respondents reported a higher rate of restructuring (32 percent) than did those in San Francisco (19 percent).

To see if certain types of organizations were more likely to consolidate than others, we looked for possible relationships between strategic restructuring experience and three characteristics of organizations: annual revenues, programmatic focus, and age. We found no significant relationship between strategic restructuring and the programmatic focus or age of an organization. However, we did find that organizations with total annual revenues of over $10 million were more likely to have strategic restructuring experience than those with revenues from $200,000 to $10 million. Given the findings from our case studies (discussed in chapters 4–8) regarding the amount of time required to consider, plan, implement, and maintain a partnership, it could be that very large organizations have the flexibility, in terms of time and money, to make a consolidation come about. Smaller organizations, by contrast, may only have the resources to make incremental changes in their structures. Larger nonprofits may also have more relationships with other organizations that have the potential to become strategic restructuring partnerships than smaller ones do. And, in a period in which managed care and other funding policies favor size, large organizations may be more appealing partners than smaller groups to other nonprofits.

Certainly, we need more information to interpret our findings and to understand how the prevalence of strategic restructuring has varied over time in the nonprofit sector as a whole, and within certain subsectors. We also need better data on the types of strategic restructuring partnerships in which nonprofits are engaging. Evidence from our survey suggests that joint programming may be the most common sort of strategic restructuring, while partnerships that involve significant integration of administrative functions, such as mergers, parent-subsidiaries, and joint ventures, are more rare. (For a more detailed description of the prevalence survey and its results, please see appendix C.)

WHAT NONPROFIT AND PHILANTHROPIC LEADERS TOLD US

Another way to assess the prevalence and importance of strategic restructuring in the nonprofit sector is to speak with leaders of larger national organizations and with researchers who have a broad perspective on the sector. (A list of the leaders we interviewed appears in Appendix E.) Eight of the 20 leaders we interviewed had observed many strategic restructuring partnerships, most often in recent years. Only Benjamin Shute of the Rockefeller Brothers Fund reported seeing fewer strategic restructuring partnerships than our survey results would lead him to believe exist. On the other hand, Jeffrey Bradach, cofounder and managing partner of The Bridgespan Group, a national nonprofit consulting firm, told us that he has been surprised that there is not more strategic restructuring activity in the nonprofit sector. He sees many opportunities for consolidation and would expect it to be more common. Three leaders felt that there has been more talk about consolidations than actual activity in this area.

The leaders generally agreed that the types of partnership we identified through the study provide a good understanding of the range that exists. The majority of respondents were quite familiar with mergers but generally less so with the other types of partnership. Lester Salamon, a professor at the Institute for Policy Studies, Johns Hopkins University, sensed that there has been an increase in the more complex types of partnerships—those that involve greater integration—but that the simpler partnerships, such as joint programming, have been around for a longer time.

We discuss the leaders' predictions about the future impact of strategic restructuring on the nonprofit sector in chapter 9. In the next chapter, we investigate why organizations decide to consolidate.

NOTES

1. Comparisons between the results of the statewide survey and of the Maryland Nonprofits member survey are only suggestive of an increase in strategic restructuring partnerships, because the samples were not identical. Moreover, although the two samples were similar in terms of the geographical distribution of organizations, they differed in terms of the size of respondent organizations. Sixty-six percent of the respondents to the statewide survey were small organizations (annual income less than $25,000) while the majority (60 percent) of respondents to the Maryland Nonprofits survey had annual budgets between $25,000 and $1 million. The Maryland Nonprofits survey also included far more large organizations (annual revenues of $1 million or more) than did the statewide survey. Thus, the differences in rates of strategic restructuring could be the result of larger organizations being more likely to consolidate than smaller ones. Additionally, information on how the two samples compare on other characteristics, such as respondent organizations' primary field of activity, was not available.

2. Strategic Solutions is directed by one of our authors.

CHAPTER 4

What Is Driving the Formation of Strategic Restructuring Partnerships?

Staff members, board members, and funders we spoke with described a great many reasons for embarking on their partnerships, but four motivations were expressed more often than others: to maintain funders' support, to save money, to capitalize on partner organizations' leadership, and to preserve or enhance their organization's reputation.[1] We explore each of these motives in this chapter.

TO MAINTAIN FUNDERS' SUPPORT

As discussed in chapter 2, some believe that organizations are mostly concerned about maintaining a predictable income stream and that this concern is behind many of the organizations' important decisions. Similarly, sociologist Roland Warren argues that organizations enter voluntarily into joint decision-making processes only when doing so is conducive to a preservation or expansion of their resources (Warren, 1972). And, indeed, in five of the six partnerships we studied in this phase of our research, worries about maintaining or building financial support seemed to have been a threshold condition for entering into serious consideration of consolidation. Although the partner organizations listed other reasons to consolidate, financial concerns seem to have been the primary motivators.

What were the nonprofits in our case studies finding—or sensing—about funders that was driving them to consider significant changes in the ways the organizations operate? Executive directors, staff members, board members, and, in some cases, funders themselves told us that institutions that give money to nonprofits are very concerned about efficiency.

Some public agencies are looking for ways to reduce the cost of contracting with nonprofits by trimming the number of contracts awarded. Patrick Tribbe, president/CEO of the Hamilton County Community Mental Health Board, which contracts with mental health agencies in Cincinnati, explained the dilemma his agency faces:

We have 45 providers but 8 or 9 of those make up the bulk of our contract money. If you take the top 9, then it probably would make up about 75 percent of our dollars that we spend. Then you've got another 35 out there that make up the other 15 percent. So what you have is a multitude of contracts that are in the $150,000–$200,000 range by some very specialty niche providers. . . . The difficulty is it costs us just as much to manage a contract that is $150,000 as it does with a $10 million agency (with a much larger contract). And they sometimes need more technical assistance. You're talking about agencies that don't have a financial officer, HR folks. . . .

It is not just public agencies that are looking for more efficient ways to dispense money; private foundations have similar concerns. Robert W. Griffith, a board member for the Speed Art Museum (which participated in the joint venture case we studied), told us that a local funder, the Fund for the Arts, scrutinizes the overhead expenses of local cultural organizations. The Fund wonders why each has to have its own pension plan and CEO, when they could consolidate and spend more money on art and less on administration.[2] (Potential dangers inherent in this perspective among some funders are discussed in chapter 9.)

Interestingly, most of the organizations we studied ultimately decided to partially or fully consolidate not because of what funders were doing at the time, but because of what they thought funders would do in the future. Margaret Harris, professor at Aston University, and her colleagues found a related motivation in her case study of a partnership of AIDS organizations in England. The study described organizations consolidating not due to organizational crises or in reaction to public policy shifts, but instead to "position themselves strategically as a group of agencies which could both take advantage of public policy shifts and be in a position to influence policy development in the future" (Harris, Harris, Hutchison, & Rochester, 1999).

In the Talbert House–Core and ACHIEVE cases, the nonprofits decided to restructure based on nonofficial signals from public funders that managed care systems might be implemented in the future and might result in a reduction in the number of contracts these funders would award. As a board member in the ACHIEVE case recalled,

It wasn't specific pressure where they came to us and said, "Look if you guys don't merge we are not going to fund you." No threats were made. They did definitely put word out that they wanted to have organizations cooperate and not have to deal with so many separate organizations. A couple of large organizations in the area had already merged, which then made us feel even more pressure to jump on the bandwagon or get left behind.

Nevertheless, several years after consolidating, none of the case study organizations that had consolidated in preparation for managed care found that their funders had switched to managed care systems. Still, those we spoke with in the STEPS–Every Woman's House and Partners for Community cases believed their efforts had been worthwhile. They felt that the efficiencies they had been able to demonstrate to funders had helped them to maintain and increase donations, grants, and contracts.

Research to date shows a lot of ambiguity about the relationship between managed care and strategic restructuring. Some organizations—like those in the Talbert House–Core and ACHIEVE cases—have made changes based on the belief that managed care will necessitate, or at least favor, larger organizations. Similarly, Fred Wulcyzn and Britany Orlebeke, researchers at Chapin Hall Center for Children at the University of Chicago, who studied four child welfare systems involved in system reform efforts based on managed care principles in 1997, found that agencies restructured to form provider networks or formed an MSO to function in their new environments (Wulczyn & Orlebeke, 2000). Restructuring, however, is not the only response to managed care. In his book on managed care in human services, Stephen Wernet describes several ways organizations are responding to managed care. Some are consolidating; others, however, are expanding on their own to provide a wider continuum of services. Still others are simply ignoring managed care because they serve niche populations and rely mostly on private funders such as the United Way (Wernet, 1999). Indeed, Keith Provan, professor of management and policy at the University of Arizona, and his research team found that strategic restructuring is not an inevitable outcome of systems that switch to managed care. In their study of a behavioral health care system in Arizona that adopted managed care strategies, the team members found no consolidation among health care networks over a four-year period (Provan, Milward, & Isett, 2001).

Certainly, more research is needed to understand when, and under what conditions, strategic restructuring is a smart response to managed care reforms or other changes in the ways funders support organizations. Several organizations that we studied appeared interested in demonstrating efficiencies through consolidation to maintain support from primary funders. But for now it remains unclear just how advantageous strategic restructuring is when it comes to maintaining funders' interest and support.

TO SAVE MONEY/BECOME MORE EFFICIENT

In his review of trends in nonprofit management, Paul Light, vice president and director of Governmental Studies and the Center for Public Service at the Brookings Institution, concludes, "Much of the 'lean and mean' rhetoric that so preoccupied private firms and government agencies during the 1980s and early 1990s has now filtered over to the nonprofit sector." Light goes on to say that those who adopt this view often advocate for a reduction (through consolidation or obliteration) in the number of nonprofits. Although they do not seem to know what the right number of organizations is, it is always less (Light, 2000).

Mark Singer and John Yankey, professors at the Mandel School of Applied Social Sciences at Case Western University, identify organizational efficiency as a strong motivation in their study of 18 nonprofit mergers (Singer & Yankey, 1991). In our survey of 192 nonprofits with strategic restructuring experience, we found that an internal decision to increase the efficiency/efficacy of their organizations was the most prevalent reason (given by 83 percent of respondents) to consolidate (Kohm, La Piana, & Gowdy, 2000). Likewise, those we interviewed for case studies generally felt that their organizations must become more efficient to withstand slow periods and attend to funders' increasing interest in cost-effectiveness. One way the organizations that we studied were pursuing this goal was through strategic restructuring. But for several, it was not the only way. Neil Tilow, president and CEO of Talbert House (the parent organization in the parent-subsidiary case study), likened his organization's programs to investments in a portfolio. Talbert eliminates programs that are not cost efficient. "In the past, we have taken on projects that have no chance of being successful financially," noted Tilow. "Before you are going to get to some good outcomes, it's going to take you a couple of years." Now Talbert only takes on programs that can show positive outcomes for clients in a relatively short period of time and can do so in a cost-efficient way. To what extent other organizations are limiting services and redirecting their attention elsewhere, because of concerns about efficiency, remains unclear. However, several national leaders in the nonprofit sector whom we interviewed about strategic restructuring expressed concern that some people in need of nonprofits' services would be hurt by a sector-wide culture focused on efficiency rather than service. (For more on nonprofit leaders' perspectives on the potential impact of strategic restructuring, see chapter 9.)

It is worth noting that, despite the apparent power of the perception of inefficiency in prompting strategic restructuring, one is hard-pressed to find evidence showing that nonprofits actually *are* inefficient. (See chapter 2 for discussion of the lack of information on the efficiency of nonprofit organizations.)

TO CAPITALIZE ON PARTNER ORGANIZATIONS' LEADERSHIP

When an organization cannot find or afford staff members—particularly senior staff—with the experience, connections, and skills that it needs, one option is to take advantage of the leadership of another organization. Interest in sharing staff was a strong motivation in several of the partnerships we studied. This interest arose, in some cases, from a sense that skilled, experienced nonprofit executives are in short supply. For example, in the STEPS–Every Woman's House case, the board of a woman's shelter went through three executive directors in three years before looking to share the well-respected director of another local agency on a part-time basis. This is not unique. As mentioned in chapter 1, a 2001 survey of more than 1,000 nonprofit executives in four U.S. cities found that most executives had been in their positions fewer than five years and had never previously headed a charity. Additionally, less than half intended to take another top job at a nonprofit organization when they left their current position (Peters & Wolfred, 2001). Although this finding does not necessarily suggest a shortage of nonprofit leaders per se, it does suggest that experienced leaders may be hard to come by.

Perhaps the most detrimental implication of the dearth of seasoned executive directors for nonprofits is the loss of the political clout and connections that such leaders can bring to an organization. As discussed earlier, such connections are vital to fundraising, and it is most often the executive director who fosters and nurtures the relationships with funders, policymakers, and other nonprofits that keep an organization strong. It takes time to develop these relationships, and such development is unlikely to occur in the first two to three years of an executive director's tenure. Affiliates of Partners for Community (PfC), the MSO that we studied, told us that one of the primary attractions of joining PfC was the association with its leaders, who had a great deal of political clout in the community.

TO PRESERVE OR ENHANCE ORGANIZATIONAL REPUTATION

When two or more organizations consolidate, they stand to benefit not only from the influence and expertise of each other's employees, but also from their partner organizations' overall standing in the community. Moreover, through strategic restructuring, they can demonstrate their interest in enhancing their efficiency. Interest in boosting organizational reputation was a key reason several of the nonprofits in our case studies tried strategic restructuring.

In the absence of strong indicators of quality or efficiency, as discussed in chapter 3, contributors often rely on an organization's reputation in making funding decisions. But this seems to create a Catch-22 situation. How does an organization gain a good or a bad reputation, if it is so difficult to assess its work? Sociologists like Paul DiMaggio and Walter Powell believe that organizations tend to mimic each other (DiMaggio & Powell, 1983). A certain approach or theory will gain currency because of novelty, because of anecdotal evidence regarding effectiveness, or simply because it seems promising. These ideas spread through consultants and employees who move from one organization to another. Organizations acquire legitimacy in the eyes of potential supporters because they have adopted whatever the new ideas are. Thus ideology rather than evidence guides organizational decisions.

Certainly, this type of mimicry is not the only basis for an organization's reputation. Some types of nonprofits—such as visual or performing arts organizations—can be more easily assessed. Contributors can see and hear what they are supporting. And many nonprofits can show progress on process goals such as moving children more quickly through foster care or providing a certain number of after-school programs for teens, even if they cannot as easily demonstrate that their clients are safer, happier, stronger, or the like.

Several organizations that we studied wanted to demonstrate, often to their funders, that they could be creative and collaborative by forming partnerships. One of the reasons the Northwest Business Development Association (NWBDA) decided to jointly operate a micro-enterprise program with Spokane Neighborhood Action Programs (SNAP) was to show the Small Business Association, which licenses NWBDA, that they could creatively address a financial void in the community.

In other partnerships we examined, organizational leaders hoped that some of their partners' reputations would rub off on them. STEPS, a substance abuse agency in Wooster, Ohio, formed an administrative consolidation with Every Woman's House (EWH), a local women's shelter. Although STEPS had stronger leadership and administrative structures than EWH had, it lacked the community recognition that EWH enjoyed. EWH benefited from the sympathy that its clients, victims of domestic violence, evoked. By contrast, some in the Wooster area blamed STEPS's clients, substance abusers, for their own problems. Through the partnership, STEPS has profited from the community's support and approval of EWH.

In another example, individuals associated with the Speed Art Museum told us that a major reason they pursued TriArt, the joint-venture gift shop and gallery, was to improve the museum's public image. They had learned from a survey they conducted that some community members felt the museum did not participate enough in the economic development of Louisville. The mayor shared this concern. When Speed received a large bequest, he suggested that the museum use it to move downtown and help revive the center city. Speed decided, instead, to stay where it was and use the funds for acquisitions and for the endowment. The TriArt partnership was a way to have a presence downtown without moving and thus appease Speed's detractors.

Yet another motivation to consolidate is simply to buy the necessary time to build organizational reputation and influence. By forming an MSO and sharing administrative responsibilities, Heriberto Flores, the executive director of the New England Farm Workers' Council, was able to free up some of his time to work on public relations and on influencing public policy. To do this, he needed to sit on various commissions and committees, which requires a great deal of time—time that is in short supply for nonprofit managers worried about facilities, fundraising, and other administrative concerns.

Looking over the most common reasons our informants gave for consolidating—whether partially or wholly—a couple of themes emerge. First, all of the motivators are either directly or indirectly related to garnering or making better use of resources. Second, many of the leaders we interviewed spoke about strategically positioning their organizations. Through strategic restructuring, they hoped to associate themselves with the best leaders, with current management strategies (i.e., collaboration), or with popular causes.

With a sense of why organizations decide to form strategic restructuring partnerships, we now examine if and how they have actually benefited from consolidating.

NOTES

1. It is worth noting that in the survey of 192 nonprofits with strategic restructuring experience conducted during Phase I of our study, we found that only 30 percent indicated that a primary reason they chose to consolidate was pressure from funders. The contrast in findings between Phases I and II could have been the result of the survey method used in the first phase, which did not probe responses as we did in the case study interviews in the second phase. It could also have resulted from the fact that we looked at only six cases in Phase II as compared to 192 in Phase I. Still another explanation might be offered based on the composition of each sample. (Neither were random samples.) Clearly, more research on the role of funders in various types of partnerships is needed.

2. Speed Art Museum is not a member of the Fund for the Arts.

CHAPTER 5

What Are the Benefits of Strategic Restructuring Partnerships?

Do organizations benefit from strategic restructuring? Although the people we spoke with were not able, in most cases, to point to hard evidence of how they directly profited from consolidation, many felt strongly that it resulted in financial savings, increased or improved services to their clientele, sharing of expertise, improved staff benefits, and enhanced organizational reputations. We explore each of these benefits in this chapter.

COST SAVINGS

About half of the organizations that we studied went into strategic restructuring with the hope of saving money. And indeed, a majority of the individuals with whom we spoke as part of the STEPS–Every Woman's House, Partners for Community, and Talbert House–Core case studies reported that their organizations had met this expectation.

Cost savings primarily resulted from volume buying, staff reduction, and sharing of employees. Perhaps the most immediate savings came from the discounts associated with volume buying. Talbert House and Core, for example, saved $100,000 on insurance in their first year.

Another source of cost savings was staff reduction, which occurred mostly through attrition rather than layoffs. None of the organizations participating in the partnerships we studied expected to lay off employees, and in a few cases the leaders explicitly promised their staff that all would keep their jobs. Jerome Weiner, president of Partners for Community, went into his partnership with a perspective similar to others with whom we spoke:

Herbie (the chairman of the MSO) and I promised no layoffs. Then I hoped that we could really live up to that, because of the significant growth. Even if we had to eliminate jobs, we could assign somebody to a new job with a higher salary. . . . You take two receptionists. One really shows promise. You put her in as a case manager and a programmer, and she blossoms.

Partners for Community was able to keep this promise initially, but after two years, they let go of a vice president and fiscal officer due to economies-of-scale issues. The only other layoff that occurred as a result of strategic restructuring, in any of the partnerships we studied, was the discharge of one of the executive directors in the ACHIEVE case, about a year into the consolidation. However, several of the organizations we studied took advantage of staff attrition. Rather than replacing a financial or human resources director, for example, an organization would share its partner organization's person. By contrast to the STEPS–Every Woman's House, Partners for Community, and Talbert House–Core cases, the ACHIEVE case did not involve significant reduction in or sharing of staff, and those involved in this restructuring did not report significant cost savings.

Although several of the case study organizations reported savings in particular areas—such as personnel or insurance—the Talbert House–Core partnership was the only case that had *documented* overall cost savings. Findings from a study of the two organizations' financial records by the University of Cincinnati confirmed that if Talbert House were to provide the services that it provided in 1999 at 1997 per-unit costs, the overall cost to the organization would have been far greater. However, the study also indicated that, although Core, the subsidiary, had demonstrated at least some cost cutting within most of its service areas, there was an overall increase in the cost of its operations due to cost increases in one particular category of service. This reduced the overall cost savings.

Assessments like this one are not common, according to John Yankey, who has conducted several studies in this area. Although 97 percent of the 23 nonprofit mergers and consolidations he studied reported that their merger or consolidation was a success, many did not conduct formal evaluations. "Conceivably, many nonprofits tie their 'feeling' of success to their motivations for entering into the merger or consolidation in the first place," note Yankey and his colleagues. "If they instinctively feel they achieved what they wanted, then they deem the alliance a success. As a result, many nonprofits may conclude that formal evaluation of success criteria determined prior to formation is not necessary" (Yankey, Wester, Koney, & McClellan, 1999). Although there are many reasons why a nonprofit may choose not to evaluate a strategic restructuring partnership—not the least of which are the difficulties and costs associated with doing so—Yankey's finding may reflect one of the basic ideas discussed in chapter 2: that nonprofits are motivated to enhance their reputation with current or potential contributors by adopting the latest management trend. The appearance of this adoption is more important than the actual effects of the strategy.

In a rare attempt to quantify the benefits of strategic restructuring (beyond a single case study), James Meier, in his evaluation of the Strategic Alliance Fund (SAF), a collaborative funding initiative managed by the United Way of New York, reported a net return of $750,000 on SAF's investment of $1 million. Most of this return resulted from new income leveraged by thirteen of the grantees. Only 40 percent came from expense-side efficiencies (Meier, 1997). Meier's findings, as well as those from our case studies, suggest that strategic restructuring partnerships may be, on average, more effective in attracting dollars than in saving them. These are important observations, given that saving money motivated many of the organizations we studied to enter partnerships.

Indeed, the smaller organizations involved in two of our cases—the ACHIEVE and the STEPS–Every Woman's House partnerships—saw an *increase* in operating costs as a result of their partnerships. In both cases, entering into the partnerships raised facilities costs. However, without the consolidation, their rental costs may still have escalated, and even become prohibitively high. For them, strategic restructuring was not intended to reduce current costs but to temper future increases in expenses. Bobbi Douglas, the executive director of STEPS and Every Woman's House, explained why both their savings and their costs rose after the organizations formed a partnership. "Our administrative costs were going to grow in terms of compliance costs and new billing/tracking systems required by the state. So our original consolidation saved cost, but we have had to add positions since that time, so our overall administrative costs have increased from five years ago."

It is also worth noting that the persistence of savings was not clear in any of our cases. Several partnerships experienced immediate windfalls by reducing facilities costs, cutting staff size, or volume buying, particularly in the area of insurance. However, none of the partnerships was old enough to demonstrate consistent savings over time. Additionally, the cost of cutting staff size is difficult to assess in the short term. Several middle- and senior-level managers reported increased stress in their jobs as a result of the partnership experience. Thus, over the long term, it is possible that in some situations strategic restructuring may result in higher staff turnover.

We need more information to understand just what the cost savings of various types of strategic restructuring are over various time periods, and whether they are sufficient to warrant consolidation efforts, if this is a primary motivation. What evidence does exist suggests that savings are possible, but certainly not guaranteed.

INCREASED OR IMPROVED SERVICES
TO CLIENTELE

Some of the benefits that the case study organizations experienced were unexpected. For example, although an interest in strengthening services was not a primary reason most of the organizations pursued strategic restructuring, many felt that it was a significant benefit of strategic restructuring, particularly in the Spokane County Microenterprise Development Program, Partners for Community, and Talbert House–Core cases.

The University of Cincinnati study of the parent-subsidiary case found that both organizations were shifting resources, providing new services, and altering existing services, and that the resource shifting allowed the agencies to increase the total number of services provided. The researchers did not have enough information to assess whether the partnership had an effect on service quality.

As noted, most partnerships rely on a feeling of progress rather than on hard evidence. In the case of Partners for Community, the organizations' leadership assumed that the partnership positively affected their clients. They felt that the clientele benefited indirectly from more staff training, an improved web site, and better technology. The microenterprise program in Spokane increased the range of services available to SNAP's low-income clientele and expanded the Northwest Business Development Association's market to include low-income clients. However, the organizations have not formally evaluated the impact of the program on participants.

The difficulty of assessing the effects of strategic restructuring partnerships on service quality reflects the more general challenge nonprofits face in demonstrating measurable outcomes. Many of the effects are indirect and appear only in the long term, defying a simple input-output equation. As Paul Light points out, "measuring the effectiveness of efforts to improve organizational effectiveness is impossible without some clearly understood definition of what effectiveness is. Given the current state of the field of nonprofit studies, that definition is still well beyond reach" (Light, 2000). In addition to this fundamental hurdle, many organizations lack the significant time and resources necessary for reliable assessments of their work.

SHARING OF EXPERTISE

Several partnerships we examined resulted in increased stores of knowledge for all of the organizations involved. This was particularly the case in the Spokane County Microenterprise Development Program, Partners for Community, and Talbert House–Core partnerships. They found that by allying with another organization, they were able to gain the expertise of some of their partner's staff members.

Combining resources through partnerships allowed some of the organizations we studied to hire and share more experienced staff members than they could have attracted on their own. For example, when STEPS's financial director left in 1998, it was possible to replace him with a finance director *and* a bookkeeper for both organizations in the partnership. Through a merger, Peninsula Children's Center, which had been operating without a financial director, gained a highly experienced one from Zonta. Similarly, Talbert House secured a medical director and a medical records director through its partnership with Core. Several leaders from the joint-programming case felt that by sharing the expertise of their individual organizations, they were able to avoid the costs of creating new capacities within each agency. As one person told us, "What has evolved is the strongest solution because we are each executing what we do anyway."

Although our case studies pointed to expertise sharing as a key benefit of some strategic restructuring partnerships, we did not find much written about this outcome in the research literature. However, some have written about a possible new wave in the way organizations operate, a wave that our case studies may reflect. These writers suggest that technology is transforming once fairly autonomous institutions into members of organizational networks and, by doing so, increasing the exchange of information and knowledge (Kushner, 1997). Organizations can share databases that are too costly to build and maintain on their own. For example, several theaters may share the data they collect on their audiences for marketing purposes, or a group of human service organizations may share data on clients who use the services of multiple agencies. E-mail makes it easier for staff to stay in contact with colleagues in separate buildings or even cities. Indeed, those in the MSO case have contemplated sharing client intake information across partnership organizations through a central database. Thus, an individual or family who enters one of the agencies need only supply information once to use the services of several agencies. Because of the possibilities of technology, partnerships are more feasible and may, in some cases, be more efficient.

IMPROVED STAFF BENEFITS

Perhaps the most easily discernable gains of strategic restructuring accrue to staff members as they become associated with, or employees of, a larger entity. This finding was most evident in the Partners for Community, Talbert House–Core, and ACHIEVE cases, in which employees—particularly those of smaller organizations—told us that their benefits improved following consolidation. Some enjoyed higher salaries as a result of the partnership, and many attained more or better insurance coverage. Only one person in the Talbert House–Core case reported that some staff complained about losing vacation days as a result of the merging of the two benefit packages.

Size also meant job security to several staff members, who felt that the partnership made their organization stronger and more likely to expand than contract. Others said that the consolidation increased staff members' opportunities to move around or up within the affiliation. Arne Kalleberg and Mark Van Buren's research corroborates the impressions of these individuals. These authors looked at the relationship between organizational size and job rewards and found that employees of large organizations obtain higher earnings and more fringe benefits and promotion opportunities than do employees of small organizations (Kalleberg & Van Buren, 1996). This result makes sense intuitively as well, since larger organizations typically have more layers of management and thus more opportunities for advancement.

ENHANCED PROFILES AND REPUTATIONS

Research reviewed by David J. Tucker and his colleagues suggests just how important partnerships may be to organizational reputation. The reviewers found that organizations that build and maintain ties with other institutions are more likely to persist than are those that do not (Tucker, Baum, & Singh, 1992). As discussed in prior chapters (see particularly chapter 2), nonprofit organizations often build legitimacy in the eyes of funders and donors not by being renegades, but by imitating the ways of other organizations with more legitimacy. A close association with a partner organization that has a good reputation would be particularly beneficial in such an environment.

Organizations involved in two of the partnerships we studied (the Partners for Community and STEPS–Every Woman's House cases) hoped to enhance their organizational profiles and reputations through strategic restructuring, and both seemed to have achieved this goal. Several persons involved felt that their organizations became more visible to the community and to the media through their partnerships. Bill Persch, director of marketing for Partners for Community, the MSO, felt it was easier to attract news coverage after the consolidation because, across all of the affiliates, they had more potentially newsworthy stories. And, by pooling funds, they had more resources to devote to marketing.

David Gadaire, executive director of CareerPoint, an affiliate of Partners for Community, described how the reputation of the lead organizations in the MSO had helped his organization.

We had an issue with one of the local politicians, who was getting some of the negative press that was being shot at our competitor and was kind of lumping us in with that. And even though we had been sending him information to say that's not the case, I'm sure the politician was just seeing that as self-serving. Jerome and Herbie [the leaders of Partners for Community] went and talked to him and explained the differences and why and how and what. . . . I'm not sure that would have happened [before CareerPoint became an MSO affiliate], especially since I'm new in this area and don't know people, and I don't carry any great impact when I call somebody.

Similarly, Lillian Cruz, the director of Humanidad Incorporated, another Partners for Community affiliate, told us that PFC has helped her organization's reputation: "I am a female-headed organization. I have to deal with gender biases. So anything that will elevate confidence in the fact that you are fully capable of doing something [is helpful.]"

Those involved in the TriArt partnership had the opposite experience. Although enhancing reputation was an important goal to 12 out of the 15 persons we spoke with regarding the joint venture, only one felt that they had reached this goal, to some extent, by showing funders and community members that the organizations could be flexible and work with other organizations. Indeed, some felt that the partnership had a *negative* effect on their organization's reputation because it ultimately failed. Others felt that the joint venture did not change the opinions of funders or others about their organization.

Executive directors seem to have a significant impact on an organization's reputation and profile in a community. However, seasoned leaders who have cultivated a reputation for trustworthiness, savvy, and knowledge of their field appear to be in short supply. An organization may spend months looking for such a director, to no avail. Or if they do find a strong candidate, they may lose out to another organization that can offer a higher salary. Strategic restructuring offers another alternative. Organizations can gain the skills and, perhaps more important, the reputation and connections of the leader of another organization through some type of affiliation.

One concern with this strategy is that an organization may also be adversely affected by the reputation of one or more of its partner(s). A director of an affiliate of Partners for Community reported that his board had some initial concern about one organization in the partnership because of some hearsay comments circulating about it. However, he noted that his board's worries dissipated after they gained some experience of the organization through the partnership. Moreover, he feels the association has actually helped his organization. He told us that it was important to be "on the right team" in his community, to be aligned with respected and well-connected leaders, and he feels his organization has done this by joining Partners for Community.

Our research and that of others suggests that organizations stand to benefit by consolidating. Improved staff benefits are perhaps the clearest

gains of strategic restructuring. However, under certain conditions, organizations can also benefit from financial savings, increased or improved
services to clientele, sharing of expertise, and enhanced reputations. Of
course, benefits must be considered in light of costs and challenges, which
we examine in the next chapter.

CHAPTER 6

What Are the Costs and Challenges of Strategic Restructuring Partnerships?

Some of the costs of strategic restructuring are obvious. Organizations can add up what they spent on hiring a consultant or a lawyer, hosting meetings, moving to a new facility, ordering new letterhead, and purchasing new software to run consolidated systems. However, the total of such out-of-pocket expenses usually does not begin to give a clear idea of what a partnership really costs. The people we interviewed stressed the hidden costs of consolidating—such as the time spent in meetings or the time spent operating two accounting systems during transitions—as often as those costs that are easily recognizable on an agency budget. In this chapter, we review financial and other costs of strategic restructuring, as well as the most difficult challenges that those in our case studies faced: lack of board and staff support, leadership problems, organizational cultural differences, identity issues, and staff turnover.

TIME COSTS

Like any reform that affects many or all aspects of an organization, strategic restructuring takes a great deal of time: time to plan and negotiate the partnership, time to get to know new colleagues, time to integrate programs and operations. Just how much time is often difficult to predict and quantify because, unlike some other types of reform, strategic restructuring requires organizations to operate in arenas where they often lack control. In other words, simple edicts from the leadership are usually not enough to ensure integration, and may in fact backfire, engendering resistance. Leaders can influence partners through building relationships, negotiations, and written agreements, but total control over partners or the partnership, most of the time, is not an option.

In most partnerships, significant amounts of time must be invested in meetings and more informal consultations to make decisions across organizations. And to optimize the chances of reaching good decisions, partners must also invest in education and information-sharing so that employees know how to make decisions and so that they have the information they need to do so (Creed & Miles, 1996; Tuite, 1972). Such investments are the transaction costs of strategic restructuring, costs organizations may not anticipate when planning partnerships.

Several interviewees in the TriArt case study described just how arduous each decision regarding the gallery and gift shop was. Major issues had to go to the boards and executive committees of the three partner organizations for consideration, which became quite cumbersome given the infrequency of these meetings. Moreover, when one group offered a revision to a proposal, it would have to go back to the other two groups. Sometimes it took three months or longer to make decisions even on well-defined issues.

Chronic underestimation of the time required for various efforts plagued several of the partnerships we studied. In the Talbert House–Core case, committees of management and front-line staff members from each organization worked to develop a unified set of policies and procedures in such functional areas as medical records, training, and risk management. Neil Tilow, the president of Talbert House, the parent organization, told us the process took more than a year longer than originally expected. However, he feels that by taking time to consider the merits of each of the organizations' policies and procedures, and to determine what might work best for both agencies, the committees eventually developed sets of rules and guidelines that were better than what either organization had originally developed. Had they known the cost of such planning—in terms of the time invested by each committee member—the partners might have at least established more realistic expectations for the process, and perhaps even reconsidered the membership or goals of the planning groups.

The results of a survey of more than 300 larger corporate mergers in recent years by Mercer Management Consulting suggest just how important taking time to integrate functions and cultures can be. Mercer found evidence that the most common reason corporate mergers fail is too much focus on the deal itself and too little attention to blending all of the systems and cultures that make the companies tick (anonymous, 1997). Although we were not able to find comparable studies in the nonprofit world, our case studies showed significant difficulties in the blending of nonprofit organizations, and many of the people we spoke with pointed to such difficulties as stumbling blocks to the success of their partnerships. (For more discussion on these challenges, see section on cultural differences later in this chapter.)

Strategic restructuring led to lost opportunities for some organizations. For example, Brion Clinkingbeard, the curator/director of exhibitions at the Kentucky Art and Craft Foundation (KACF), felt that the time and other resources spent on the exhibitions that KACF produced for the TriArt gallery would have been better spent on shows at KACF's main site. He believed the KACF staff could have done a better job on the exhibitions in the larger space at KACF, and his institution could have kept all of the proceeds rather than splitting them with the partner organizations.

Insufficient attention to time expenditures began early in most of the partnerships we studied. In our interviews, we asked people whether their organizations considered how they could have employed the considerable resources spent on their partnerships—such as staff time—in other, potentially more profitable ways than strategic restructuring. Few reported that such weighing of options occurred. Instead, the consolidation idea emerged early on and dominated discussions. It is worth emphasizing that, as discussed in this and other chapters in this book, it is difficult to do any kind of definitive cost-benefit analysis of strategic restructuring versus other strategies. Both unexpected costs and benefits emerge as a partnership progresses. However, it seems notable that this stage of planning was cursory or nonexistent in most of the partnerships we examined. The minimal consideration of options may also suggest (as discussed in chapter 2) that some organizations were more interested in showing funders that they were pursuing a popular management strategy than in assessing the costs and benefits of various strategies.

FINANCIAL COSTS (AND THEIR IMPACT)

Plenty of researchers have looked at cost-benefit equations in mergers among for-profit companies. The findings of many of these studies may serve as a warning to nonprofits considering consolidation. For example, Alexandra Reed Lajoux and J. Fred Weston reviewed 19 studies of long-term, post-merger performance of for-profit companies. They concluded that, although some studies show positive effects, most reveal that mergers impair the value of a corporation (whether measured by share price or other indicators) for a variety of reasons, including inexperience, unrealistic optimism about potential synergies, and poor post-merger integration (Lajoux & Weston, 1998). Although such findings are important for those in the nonprofit world to consider, they provide only a crude understanding of how partial and full consolidations among nonprofit organizations affect their cost-benefit equations, which, as discussed earlier in this book, are quite complex and difficult to measure.

Perhaps easiest to determine (if not always to accurately predict) are the costs of strategic restructuring among nonprofits that directly affect the bank balance of organizations. Most of the people we interviewed as part of the TriArt, Spokane County Microenterprise Development Program, and STEPS–Every Woman's House cases spoke about the direct financial impact of their partnerships. And when the impact was high, many took notice—more notice than when time costs grew. For example, although TriArt interviewees varied in their emphasis on the importance of generating revenue, all agreed that the venture ended up costing money rather than making it. Each time the partners made loans to the venture, they became more skittish. As with many fledgling business ventures, it was not clear to the organizations when they needed to invest more resources and when to cut costs.

A benefit of strategic restructuring, as discussed in chapter 5, can be an upgrade in facilities, equipment, or the expertise of personnel. These benefits, however, often come at a price. The building that STEPS and Every Woman's House share, for example, proved to be more complicated and expensive to operate than they had predicted. Eventually they decided a new expense—the salary of a director of operations—was necessary to deal with facilities issues.

LOW BOARD AND STAFF MORALE

Evidence from for-profit mergers shows that they can undermine staff morale, which in turn can hurt operations. Sue Cartwright and Cary L. Cooper report that "Instead of achieving the projected economies of scale, mergers have become associated with lowered productivity, worse strike records, higher absenteeism and poorer accident rates rather than greater profitability" (Cartwright & Cooper, 1996).

Similarly, Martha Golensky and Gerald L. DeRuiter found that in two of three nonprofit merger case studies they conducted,

The lack of communication with staff early on about the merger and the manner in which staff cuts have been carried out have resulted in serious morale problems that must be resolved for the merged corporations to be able to focus fully on planning for the future. (Golensky & DeRuiter, 1999)

With such indications about the importance of attending to employee morale in consolidations, those considering strategic restructuring need a clear understanding of the extent, nature, and impact of partnerships on nonprofit organizations—particularly because many nonprofits cannot boost morale with wages and benefits packages. Instead, they often rely on employee commitment to an issue or cause. If a consolidation damages this commitment, the impact may be even more detrimental for nonprofits than it is for for-profit organizations.

Winning staff and board support and maintaining or boosting their morale throughout the process were especially significant challenges in the ACHIEVE and TriArt cases. Early on in the TriArt partnership, staff and board members had concerns about the viability of the plan. Some felt that it would be difficult to make such a venture profitable. Others worried that the gallery and gift shop did not appropriately reflect their organization's mission. Several people, including the executive directors of the three partner organizations, felt that staff and board members were not involved enough in the planning of the effort and that the project was being imposed upon them. Brion Clinkingbeard, curator/director of exhibitions at the Kentucky Art and Craft Foundation (KACF), told us that, after TriArt opened, KACF staff members were producing one or two extra exhibitions with the same human resources and no extra pay.

Even in more successful partnerships, senior management staff often described workloads that grew heavier as partnerships arose and developed. Among those we interviewed, senior staff felt most impacted (and often most burdened) by the partnerships.

- Fifty-seven percent of senior staff reported a change in title, while only 29 percent of executive directors and 14 percent of other staff did.

- Fifty-nine percent of senior staff reported a change in job responsibilities, while only 32 percent of executive directors and 9 percent of other staff did.

- Board members and executive directors tended to assess the overall success of their respective partnerships higher than did senior staff. Sixty-two percent of board members and 73 percent of executive directors rated their partnerships as successful or very successful, while only 53 percent of senior staff did.

- Senior staff were the least personally satisfied of the three groups: 47 percent of senior staff said they were satisfied or very satisfied with the partnership, while 73 percent of executive directors and 64 percent of board members did.[1]

The people we interviewed also told us that senior and middle managers were more worried about losing their jobs or losing influence within the organization than were other staff. Although the partnerships we examined did not result in many layoffs, some middle-management people chose to leave due to increased pressure or the changing nature of their jobs or of organizational cultures.

LEADERSHIP PROBLEMS

A host of leadership problems arose in the partnerships we studied. Many concerned leaders struggling to strike a balance between strong, authoritative decision making and responsiveness to staff members' concerns—both of which appeared important to making partnerships work.

To avoid damaging staff morale with the appearance that one organization was dominating the other, some partnerships took pains to share leadership. Jean Spurr, director of human resources for ACHIEVE, the merged organization we studied, told us, "We had two HR directors for a year; we had two development directors. We had two school directors. We had two mental health directors. We had two executive directors. Because I don't think anybody wanted to fire anybody as a result of the merger, so in the absence of wanting to fire somebody, I think there could have been a clear plan about what to do with all these extra people." The outcome, as Spurr suggests, was a lot of confusion about who *really* was in charge of what.

Indeed, the thorniest leadership problems in most of the partnerships we studied related to sharing power. Allan Cowen, president and CEO of the Fund for the Arts, which supported the TriArt joint venture, felt that the partnership suffered from "floating accountability." Similarly, Mary Miller, executive director of the Kentucky Art and Craft Foundation, described TriArt as a sometimes unwanted stepchild. "We all were busy carrying out our own separate missions," said Miller, "and sometimes there just wasn't room for TriArt. Sometimes things were just ignored or pushed to the back burner."

Sharing leadership was not the only leadership problem. Even when everyone agreed on who was in charge, staff often had trouble adjusting to the differing management styles of leaders in their partner organizations. This was particularly pronounced in the Talbert House–Core case, in which staff from one organization sometimes had supervisors from the other. The relationship between the two directors was also fairly complex. Neil Tilow, the president and CEO of Talbert House, the parent organization, explained that he sees Core as not just a *subsidiary* but also a *customer,* because it is paying Talbert for administrative support. However, the executive director of Core is also an employee who reports to the executive director of Talbert. Given the complexity of the relationship between the organizations and among the individuals within them, knowing what protocol to follow in any situation can be difficult. For example, Tilow told us that early on in the partnership he made a unilateral decision about a benefits policy. Paul Guggenheim, Core's director, complained. Tilow recognized his mistake and told the insurance brokers to hold off while Core considered the impact of the policy on its employees. Tilow has had to learn that certain decisions will take longer with subsidiaries, because more people have to be involved.

Gail Switzer, the former executive director of ACHIEVE, spoke of the difficulties of finding oneself, post-merger, at the helm of a much larger organization.

One of the differences in managing a big organization versus a small one is you really need to look at results more objectively rather than work with people and know all the nuances of why the results aren't there. You can't possibly have your hands on everything the way you did before. So results are what have to be important.

Maintaining a positive public image and close ties with funding sources is critical to the survival of organizations that depend on large grants and contracts. Leaders may delegate more of the operation of the organization to staff members to free up time for external relations. Neil Tilow of Talbert House has delegated a great deal of authority and now spends about 50 percent of his time on outside activities rather than on those related to the day-to-day operations of the organization. Although he feels that he is spending his time wisely, he also expressed concern about not knowing, off the top of his head, the particulars about various programs and operations. Prior to the partnership, he used to know everyone at Talbert by name. Afterward, he joked, he hardly knew where all thirty locations of the parent and its subsidiaries were.[2]

On the opposite end of the spectrum, Roland Kushner warns of the dangers of directors spending too much time looking at the environment and maintaining partnerships rather than focusing on the operations of their own organizations. "[Networks] can also create new demands on managerial attention and resources. . . . By directing attention outward, they can contribute to diminished organizational focus. A wider scope of management responsibility can reverse efficiency benefits which may have been gained" (Kushner, 1997). The leaders of Partners for Community addressed this concern by dividing up internal and external responsibilities between the MSO's two primary leaders. Jerome Weiner oversees internal operations, while Herbie Flores fosters and maintains the relationships with funders and politicians that are so important to PfC and its affiliates.

To step back from the minutia of daily organizational life, as Switzer and Tilow described, executive directors must delegate more. However, several staff members we spoke with complained that, despite the fact that their directors had delegated more responsibilities to them, they had not been given sufficient authority or information to carry out the new tasks. Lara Ginsburg, operations director for STEPS, felt she could do more if she had access to departmental budgets or goals to use as guides in planning. Without this information, she felt she spent a lot of her time putting out fires rather than preventing them. David Eve, vice president for information and technology for Partners for Community (the MSO), had a similar view, and spoke of PfC's efforts to make budget information available to staff so that they could make certain decisions, leaving management staff to focus on other concerns:

If they [line staff] know the numbers, if they know their budget, what they have authority to spend, and they know the expectations, then they are in the best position to determine when they need to buy more computer paper and more pencils and more cups.

Directors and staff can more easily adapt to changes when a high degree of trust wards off doubt and worries. Switzer described how she struggled to lead in an atmosphere of distrust in which the impact of seemingly minor mistakes became magnified:

For the first six months, any incompetence was seen [by former Zonta staff] as a plot against them. So if we sent out a newsletter and mentioned PCC more times then we mentioned Zonta, that was a deliberate plot. If we forgot to ask them something, it was a deliberate plot.

By contrast, staff members we spoke to as part of the Partners for Community study emphasized their respect for their own director and that of their partner organization. This trust preceded the birth of the MSO, due to the leaders' reputation in the community, and continued since the leaders spent a great deal of time talking to staff about the partnership and their particular roles in it. (See the next chapter for more on the role of trust in strategic restructuring partnerships.)

Much of the research and theory-based literature related to strategic restructuring among nonprofits focuses on how organizations decide to enter a partnership and on how they close the deal. We found much less examination of what they do afterward, such as how organizations deal with leadership problems. Also, as the previous discussion demonstrates, some of the leadership issues that arise in these partnerships are not particular to strategic restructuring, but are those that occur whenever an organization grows or changes, for whatever reason.

ORGANIZATIONAL CULTURAL DIFFERENCES

People in all of the case studies spoke of cultural differences and clashes between partner organizations; this was especially true for the most integrated partnerships, the Talbert House–Core and ACHIEVE cases. "Cultural differences" seemed to be a catchall term to refer to a variety of problems. An organization's culture, according to those we interviewed, is some combination of policies and procedures, professional philosophies, employee dress, meeting frequency and attendance, and the types of relationships that exist between and among management and staff. Research on corporate mergers reflects some of these findings. Cartwright and Cooper, for example, note that an organization is shaped by its history, its ownership, its size, the nature of its business, and its founders and leaders (Cartwright & Cooper, 1996).

However, the most important aspects of culture, according to many in our study, are the ways in which decisions are made. Who is informed about decisions? Who is included in making them? Who has access to decision makers? How long do decisions take? Are decisions made behind closed doors? Through multiple meetings? Through consensus, vote, or executive fiat? Who are the ostensible and de facto decision makers?

Despite (or perhaps because of) the pervasiveness of organizational culture, it tends to be invisible to an organization's staff and board until it butts up against another culture. "You don't realize you have a culture until something like this happens," noted Gail Switzer of ACHIEVE. Perhaps because of culture's invisibility prior to consolidation, many cultural clashes emerged unexpectedly. Some individuals we interviewed guessed (or hoped) that, because their organization and their partner served similar clients, or because they shared similar approaches or philosophies in their work, cultural differences would not be a problem. But despite such similarities, other aspects of culture clashed. For example, although the people we spoke with in the Talbert House–Core and ACHIEVE cases spoke of philosophical differences among professionals, the more invisible aspects of culture—such as how decisions were made—were what tended to wreak havoc on the partnerships.

Reflecting on the ACHIEVE merger, Patricia Gardner, former development director for ACHIEVE, wondered whether organizational cultural integration might be a more significant issue in nonprofit consolidations than in for-profit ones. "We are not here for a business reason," she stressed. "We are here because we like the people. We like the clients. We like the atmosphere, and they [the boards] didn't take into consideration cultural issues when they made some management decisions."

Cultures meld gradually under most conditions, and most will change only at a glacial pace when organizations and staff are distant from one another. Bill Persch of Partners for Community described how certain programs of the affiliated organizations have maintained their "traditional identities" because they are more geographically removed from "the center of corporate activity." Similarly, Gardner of ACHIEVE told us,

If you look at an organization chart, you would be able to say this should all be able to be managed by one person, until you met the people and had to drive the distance [between sites]. In theory it was good, but in practice it wasn't going to work.

Based on the idea that the two sites (formerly two organizations) would come together more if they knew each other better, Switzer, who formerly directed PCC, began spending two days a week at the site that was formerly Zonta. But cultural barriers persisted. As one board member described it, even though Switzer kept her door open when she was at her second office,

Nobody ever came in. It's awkward. They didn't really know her and what were they gonna do, go up and just shoot the breeze? It just didn't work. And then it became quite . . . inefficient, and she was wasting tons of time going back and forth, and so that kind of fell by the wayside.

Switzer's experience suggests that physical presence by a leader is not enough to build a relationship with a staff. Had Switzer been able to spend her time at the Zonta site walking around and getting to know people, she might have formed relationships with some of the staff at that site. This would have required a tremendous amount of the leader's time, which is usually in short supply.

Michael Hannan and John Freeman offer an explanation for why an organization's "repertoire of routines" is so difficult to change. They describe how organizations develop practices and customs to ensure reliable performance. Soon those within the organization are dedicated to the predictability of these routines and do their best to maintain the status quo. This may explain why staff and board members in our case studies who believed in the logic of a consolidation had trouble dealing with the changes in operations and programs that followed. Hannan and Freeman maintain that staff resistance can delay adaptations to changing environmental conditions to such an extent that an environmental fluctuation may be over before any organizational change has occurred. They argue that, because of staff members' defense of current policies and procedures (and presumably other aspects of culture), new organizational forms come about more often from the creation of new organizations with new structures than from the restructuring of existing organizations (Hannan & Freeman, 1984).

The degree of organizational cultural integration in a partnership, as Gardner suggested, depends on the particular personalities involved. Some staff and board members from Zonta described PCC staff who had been around for many years as having formed a clique into which others were not welcome. However, informants singled out other individuals, from both organizations, who were able to bridge the gap by doggedly pursuing a partnership with their new colleagues through meetings, phone calls, and proposing collective work. In the parent-subsidiary case, staff members were, to some extent, forced to cooperate. Employees from each organization worked together on committees. They were charged with determining a new, consolidated structure for a program or hammering out joint policies and procedures. Through such close and constant interaction, some barriers came down and some hard-won respect was granted.

A few people, including two executive directors, felt that, although cultural *clashes* must be addressed, cultural *differences* do not necessarily represent problems in need of solutions. Gail Switzer concluded,

There will never be one culture in an agency, just like each of our classrooms is very different depending on the personalities there, and maybe you need to pick out one or two key things that you insist on across the agency but otherwise not worry so much about things being the same.

Jerome Weiner of Partners for Community also thought that a certain degree of cultural integration as well as difference was acceptable—maybe even preferable.

Something that I found in the three-and-a-half years is if you set the tone, and you let people know what the vision of the organization is, and they share that vision, they'll adapt to corporate culture. The one thing we learned is that that was the least of our problems, and we have had so much fun enjoying each other's cultures, and now we have a very multicultural corporation.

IDENTITY ISSUES

Our research and that of others suggests that strategic restructuring can be, and often is, a counter-intuitive step for organizations that spend much of their energy and time on maintaining their identity. By doing so, they build the loyalty of those inside and outside the institution. Full consolidations require stakeholders to transfer that loyalty to a new institution. Partial consolidations ask them to somehow parse or spread their loyalty. Organizations resist such difficult and even distasteful work unless they feel they have good, perhaps vital, reasons for doing so.

This challenge relates to, but appears to transcend, cultural issues. Whereas culture is mostly an internal concern, organizational identity is a public asset. It attracts staff, board members, clients, and funders to particular organizations. Some informants likened the power of organizational identity to what those in the corporate world call brand loyalty. Such loyalty may be particularly important for nonprofits, whose funders and donors, lacking clear indications of an organization's value, base their contribution decisions on a sense of its legitimacy. (See discussion on organizational legitimacy in chapter 2.)

People we spoke with in the Talbert House–Core case study told us an important reason they decided not to fully merge was to preserve the brand names, and thus brand identity, that the organizations had cultivated in their communities. "Talbert would be like General Motors and orchestrate all these different brand names," said Robert T. Lameier, a board member for Core, Talbert's subsidiary. "There is some value in brand names, and when you think of severely mentally handicapped people you should be thinking of Core."

Maintaining brand names, according to Neil Tilow of Talbert House, also helped to ease the fears of some competitors. Tilow wanted to prevent other agencies from worrying that Talbert House might become too large, and complaining to funding sources about it. Tilow told us, "I have to do business with these people all of the time, so I didn't want to do something that more or less would make them cautious or anxious about dealing with Talbert House and Core."

Ironically, partial consolidations appear to confuse organizational identity as well as help preserve it. "Agencies have histories and reputations, good and bad," noted Patrick Tribbe, who represents one of the major funders of Talbert House and Core, "and all those things get on the line when you bring them together." Lillian Cruz, executive director of Humanidad Incorporated, spoke about her organization's concerns that it would lose its identity—which had been heavily marketed to its own staff, clients, and their families—due to the affiliation with an MSO. Indeed, Clyde Miller, a Talbert staff member, said even he and other staff members remained confused about their organizational identity post-consolidation. "It is a strange hybrid," he noted. "Some parts of Talbert House and Core are really together, and another part of it may not be."

The most visible symbol of an organization's identity is its name, and often the most heated battles in strategic restructuring occur over name changes. A board member of the merged ACHIEVE said that some staff threatened to quit if certain names were chosen. When the organizations' names remain after strategic restructuring, as in a parent-subsidary partnership, the names' symbolic weight is often evident. Paul Guggenheim, executive director of Core, showed us a new best-practice manual. Staff from both organizations created the manual, but in many places on the publication, including the cover, only Talbert House is mentioned. Guggenheim noted that these were small mistakes, which did not happen often but tended "to infuriate staff because they feel they are being ignored or absorbed."

Sometimes staff and board members' sense of their organization's identity, and of their own identity as part of it, are so strong that their allegiance is difficult to alter or sever. Shirley Brice Heath and Milbrey McLaughlin conclude, based on their research on youth-serving organizations, that, "Any collaboration of personnel, services, and resources threatens an organization's sense of self and raises defenses against adaptation to the exigencies of limited resources and shifting demographics" (Heath & McLaughlin, 1993).

Ron Holtman, a board member for STEPS, attested to the strength of organizational identity when he told us that the administrative consolidation could have failed on "partisan" grounds due to turf issues. "It took a fair amount of confidence and assurance between various board members to set aside their parochial concerns and recognize that consolidation was in their respective agency's best interests."

Margaret Harris and her colleagues, however, found that concerns about advancing an organization's mission *can* override worries about maintaining organizational identity. In their case study of an alliance among nonprofits, they found that "the drive to position themselves strategically was, for at least some of the consortium agencies, a factor which more than counterbalanced their wish to retain their autonomy and their local and regional focus."

STAFF TURNOVER

We include a brief discussion on staff turnover here even though it is not similar to the costs and challenges discussed so far, in that turnover is not necessarily a challenge. Some partnerships do not involve any layoffs. Others form, at least in part, to reduce staff (and thus cost), yet reductions occur with minimal lasting or widespread effects. Indeed only 7 out of our 65 interviewees described staff turnover as a challenge, and in our earlier survey of 192 nonprofits that had strategic restructuring experience, only 10 percent indicated that layoffs posed a significant problem. However, because layoffs are highly visible in corporate mergers, many facing strategic restructuring in the nonprofit world have concerns about this possibility. So to provide an understanding of the role of turnover in some strategic restructuring partnerships, we describe why and how the turnover in our case studies occurred.

Some of the layoffs and resignations that our case study participants described were indirect effects of consolidation. Strategic restructuring led to changes in leadership, which in turn led to changes in philosophy or structure, which finally resulted in voluntary and involuntary staff turnover within organizations.

Some staff left after consolidation not because of a new supervisor with a new style, but because the organization itself had changed and was no longer the type of place in which they wanted to work. "I think some people left because they liked a small nonprofit and that kind of delivery, and suddenly we were looking like a big corporation with lots of grassroots offices and tentacles out there," noted Jerome Weiner of Partners for Community. "And I think some people may have just had difficulty with the philosophy that we shouldn't be big." Others, according to some of the people we interviewed, could not handle the increased workload or working across organizations.

Despite "no layoff" declarations by executive directors, staff members in most of the cases studied feared that to realize economies of scale, their organizations eventually would reduce staff. It is interesting to note these fears, given that, for the most part, the managers of the partnerships appear to have kept their promises. Two years into the MSO, Partners for Community let go a fiscal officer to reduce redundancy and realize efficiencies. Talbert House and Core let some positions go through attrition. The ACHIEVE merger, however, involved only one layoff, the executive director of one of the original organizations. Indeed, several informants, including staff members, complained that, as a result of a staunch position against layoffs, ACHIEVE became too top heavy.

Our interviews revealed that, although staff turnover was not so great a cost of strategic restructuring as we might have expected, staff changes (from other causes) created challenges for consolidation efforts. For example, the staff at SNAP spent the better part of a year planning a joint micro-enterprise program with the executive director of Northwest Business Development Association. When the NWBDA let this director go, SNAP learned that he had never told his board about the partnership. Luckily, detailed minutes of all the planning meetings had been kept, and the board decided to go ahead with the program. As discussed earlier, the STEPS leadership became concerned when the organization's partner, Every Woman's House, went through three directors in three years. Their worries about being affiliated with an unstable organization led them to consider sharing their executive director with EWH. And the already faltering TriArt partnership became even more tenuous when one of the executive directors of a partner organization left. Her replacement did not share her enthusiasm for the joint venture idea, and shortly after this transition the partnership folded.

Although some books and articles offer advice about handling layoffs and turnover in nonprofit consolidations, we found little research-based literature on the topic. Martha Golensky and Gerald DeRuiter describe how sensitive the issue of turnover can be, in their description of a nonprofit merger they studied:

> The decision to issue pink slips to all line staff and require them to reapply for their positions, done out of a misguided belief this might engender loyalty to the new corporation, exacerbated the situation, and staff turnover has been very high throughout the implementation period. (Golensky & DeRuiter, 1999)

This finding, along with our own observations, seems to point to the importance of recognizing and dealing sensitively with staff concerns about layoffs—even when few, if any, will occur. Additionally, organizations should be prepared for staff choosing to leave as a result of restructuring-related changes, and for the effects of natural turnover on partnerships.

The potential costs of strategic restructuring are considerable. However, those who have managed such partnerships have found ways to optimize success. We review success factors in strategic restructuring in the next chapter.

NOTES

1. These figures could result at least in part from the fact that over 50 percent of the senior staff we interviewed were associated with the merger and joint-venture cases, which were less successful than the others.

2. Talbert added another subsidiary after Core.

CHAPTER 7

What Factors Contribute to Successful Strategic Restructuring Partnerships?

Our case study participants agreed more often about why their organizations pursued strategic restructuring and what the effects were than about what made them work. However, a few success factors emerged across the cases: research and planning, openness and communication, trust, and strong staff teams. We discuss each of these factors in this chapter.

RESEARCH/PLANNING

Some research on structural change in organizations points to the importance of planning and the need for resources to do it effectively. Michael Hannan and John Freeman suggest that, because large organizations often have more resources than small ones, the rate of achieving structural change may increase with size (Hannan & Freeman, 1984). Twombly adds that larger organizations' resources tend to buffer them from dramatic environmental changes and thus allow more time to reorganize to deal with threats that can overcome smaller organizations (Twombly, 2000). This observation may explain why we found strategic restructuring most prevalent among organizations with annual revenues of $10 million or more. (See chapter 4 for more on the prevalence of strategic restructuring.)

The importance of planning came through in several of our case studies. Those involved in the TriArt, Talbert House–Core, and ACHIEVE cases advised anyone considering strategic restructuring to first explore all options and the implications of those options—and to do so thoroughly. Indeed, several people in the TriArt and ACHIEVE studies questioned whether their organizations would have proceeded with strategic restructuring had they done more research into the potential costs and how these stacked up against potential benefits. Several also thought a deeper consideration of how the partnership would or would not advance the partners' organizational missions might have helped them to make better decisions about whether and how to move forward.

Staff and board members we spoke with had less to say on how to go about research than on its general importance. Several thought that a consultant with expertise in consolidation might have helped them. Only the Spokane County Microenterprise Development Program, the joint-programming partnership (perhaps the most common type of strategic restructuring partnership among nonprofits), had looked for and found a similar program on which to model efforts. Jerome Weiner, the chief executive officer of Partners for Community, searched for other MSOs in the human services sector but only found a few, apparently unsuccessful, models in the mental health field.

The planning of the other four partnerships involved little to no research. In the administrative consolidation, parent-subsidiary, and joint-venture cases, interviewees felt that they had embarked on something novel and had to plan without the benefit of others' experiences.

There was not a great deal of agreement across cases as to the number and kinds of stakeholders who should be involved in planning a partnership. However, interviewees generally felt that involving staff and board members was a good way to inform the consolidation process and secure support. Several people recommended that, after research has been conducted, organizations set realistic, clearly defined, and widely understood (among staff and board) expectations for the partnership. A few also felt that the ramifications of the partnership for specific departments and individual staff members should be clearly communicated. By doing so, they believed, organizations could more easily win the support of key stakeholders. Partners for Community seems to have spent more time on such activities than had the other organizations we examined, and did enjoy strong support from staff members. Had board and staff members in the ACHIEVE or TriArt cases been satisfied concerning the rationale and approach prior to implementation, the organizations might have better withstood stormy episodes, such as when the leaders of ACHIEVE, the merged organization, were trying to figure out the right staff configuration for the new entity.

OPENNESS AND COMMUNICATION

Surfacing the truths about your organization and that of your partner(s) may not be pleasant, but is important to the success of strategic restructuring, according to our interviewees. In a published summary of his strategic restructuring experience, Jerome Weiner recalled,

We encouraged the hard questions of each other and our respective management and line staffs concerning agency strengths/weaknesses, assets and potential liabilities and especially any skeletons that might be hidden in our closets and not readily visible on a financial statement.

Similarly, Gail Switzer of ACHIEVE advised others planning partnerships to

listen to what people are saying and don't assume they are saying what you want them to say. So if you're working with people from different agencies or different thought processes, cultures, don't minimize the differences between what they are saying.

One ACHIEVE staff member felt that the management did not allow staff to express their concerns and frustrations enough, and that, had they done so, this might have served as a sort of safety valve, allowing the merger time to solidify without individuals undermining it. Other organizational leaders described how their partnerships improved when they listened to a variety of people—funders, staff members, board members, and sometimes clients. "One thing that was really stressed is that if you get people involved, and incorporate ideas from a diverse group of individuals, you end up with something that is better," said Ray Lancaster of the Spokane County Microenterprise Development Program, "because we all come from our own little place, and we can only see things from our own eyes."

Interorganizational decision making works best, according to Matthew Tuite, when all of the parties involved are willing to participate and have the information they need to do so (Tuite, 1972). This involves a great deal of communication at each step. Individuals need information to convince them to join in a change process, and then need information to coordinate or meld work across organizations. Kate Cowin and Geoff Moore report on research on mergers in the United Kingdom's nonprofit sector from 1988 to 1993, and conclude that a merger can be an effective strategy for nonprofit organizations if it has been undertaken willingly with a shared vision between the partners of what the merger will achieve (Cowin & Moore, 1996).

On the other hand, several people in our case studies agreed that at some point one or more people—usually the executive director(s)—need to show everyone where the partnership is going and lead the organization(s) in that direction. In their opinion, discussion without leadership (action) can be just as frustrating to staff, and to the partnership itself, as autocratic rule. Michael Oberdoerster, medical director for both Talbert and Core in the parent-subsidiary case, complained about spending too much time in meetings: "We are sitting in meetings arguing in this room about one hundred dollars, and we've already wasted the hundred dollars arguing about small-ticket items. . . . " Gail Switzer, the former executive director of ACHIEVE, pointed to a similar problem when she reflected, "I think I tried to make them [her staff] feel that their vision was the same as my vision rather than just saying this is my vision, [and] if you don't like it, maybe this isn't the right place for you." Heriberto Flores, chair of Partners for Community, did take this approach with staff. In one-on-one meetings and group discussions, he and Jerome Weiner said, "This is where we are, and this is where we are going. You can help us to build the bridge."

TRUST

Implicit in people's suggestions about openness and communication, as well as about strong leadership, seemed to be the importance of trust. David Campbell examined decision-making conditions in interorganizational restructuring and found that, in his case studies, trust was not a necessary condition for restructuring but that, without it, individuals were more ambivalent about entering a partnership (Campbell, 2000). Similarly, Walter Powell stresses that all types of transaction costs within and across organizations decrease as trust grows. It is simply easier and faster to deal with people whom you trust than with those you do not (Powell, 1996). Lauren William's research on the interpersonal aspects of strategic alliance decisions points to the evolution of trust in organizational partnerships from quid-pro-quo exchanges to shared purposes and searches for positive sum outcomes (Williams, 2000).

If engendering trust is important in strategic restructuring partnerships, it would be helpful to know just what trust is and how it grows. Based on a review of research on trust among people and groups, Aneil K. Mishra defines trust as "one party's willingness to be vulnerable to another party based on the belief that the latter party is (a) competent, (b) open, (c) concerned, and (d) reliable" (Mishra, 1996). Douglas Creed and Raymond Miles posit that the essential ingredients for trust are a predisposition to trust, characteristic similarity among parties, and prior experiences of reciprocity on the part of all parties (Creed & Miles, 1996). Powell emphasizes that the building of trust happens over a period of time and must be reinforced through regular dialogue (Powell, 1996). According to these definitions, organizations that are similar in some ways and already have established working relationships may be most suitable as partners. However, strategic restructuring requires a level of vulnerability probably not previously experienced by organizations first entering partnerships.

Our case studies show that as organizations experience their partners as competent, open, concerned, and reliable, trust grows, and appears to grow more quickly, with more opportunities for stakeholders in each organization to get to know each other. Russell Peguero-Winters, director of case management at Core Behavioral Health Centers, was a member of a group of Core and Talbert employees charged with integrating the counseling programs of the two organizations. He described the experience as stressful, with committee members defending their organization's clinical philosophies and ways of operating. However, discussions became more amicable as time went on, because, in Winters' opinion, committee members became more familiar with each other. By the end of the process, they had a certain degree of respect for each other as professionals, which "had to be earned."

STRONG STAFF TEAMS

Lauren Williams found in her research on nonprofit alliances, as we had in our case studies, that individuals can make or break partnerships. However, she noticed that most of the literature on partnerships focuses on structure, strategy, and economic factors but not at all on the people "behind the deal," a topic that attracts much attention in actual alliances (Williams, 2000). We too had difficulty finding research or theory on how individuals affect consolidations. We did find a study by Samuel Goldman and William Kahnweiler that focused on 92 nonprofit executive directors who engaged in interorganizational collaborations. They found that directors who were predisposed to perceive their collaborations as successful were extroverts who could work in ambiguous and multiple roles within their organization (Goldman & Kahnweiler, 2000). However, a director's perception that his or her collaboration was successful might not reflect whether it actually was successful. Moreover, Campbell found that the champions of partnerships need not be executive directors (Campbell, 2000). Perhaps more instructive is Pennie Foster-Fishman and her colleagues' review of literature about the factors that impact staff attitudes in human services toward various types of reform. These reviewers conclude that, in "organizations where policies and practices promote employee autonomy and control, staff are more likely to have the capacity to adopt new roles and responsibilities and to view the reforms as possible and desirable" (Foster-Fishman, Salem, Allen, & Fahrbach, 1999).

This finding clearly reflects our own. However, staff empowerment appears to be too simple a prescription. The characteristics of individuals involved mattered as well. This success factor appeared in the majority of interviews in all but the TriArt and ACHIEVE cases, which, perhaps significantly, were the least successful partnerships.

Many of the people we spoke with pointed to individuals who were champions of the partnership. In most cases, the individuals were the executive directors of the organizations involved. Critical to the progress of the partnership were the champions' abilities to bring parties together, to make hard decisions, to win the respect of partner organizations, to make mission-based rather than ego-based decisions, to work many hours, and to obtain valuable input from staff. Champions also tended to have had a substantial tenure at their organizations.

Others spoke of the necessity of having flexible staff members who have faith in their organizational leaders and in the partnership in general. These employees seem to be particularly important when the partnership is still relatively new and systems of cooperation have not yet been well established. "There are people within various organizations that have very collaborative kinds of spirits," noted Pam McClain, a vice president for Talbert House, "and they're great facilitators and that may be their individual skill, but you need the systems really in an infrastructure. . . . I think that too often it rests on the people versus the system." She explained that there were two directors at Core, Talbert's subsidiary, whom she interacted with the most. One relationship has worked well because, in McClain's opinion, she and that director speak a lot and have collaborative spirits. However, it has been more difficult with the other director. "He was a very different kind of person, but there was no system to make it work overall, so it became very personality dependent."

The lessons from people we talked with are clear: to optimize the success of strategic restructuring, not only do organizations need the right people involved, but also those people need access to information to make critical decisions. Moreover, staff autonomy should be balanced by strong and clear leadership. And perhaps most important of all, a partnership works best when it is carefully planned and everyone starts out trusting its leaders.

We turn now from a consideration of strategic restructuring's impact on individual nonprofits to the question of how strategic restructuring might affect the nonprofit sector in the years to come.

CHAPTER 8

The Future Impact of Strategic Restructuring on the Nonprofit Sector

The case studies and prevalence studies helped us to understand what is happening now in the area of strategic restructuring among nonprofits, but gave us little sense of the future. For that, we turned to 20 leaders in the nonprofit and philanthropic sectors, people who have both a long and a broad view of the sector through their work as national funders, heads of national associations of nonprofits, researchers, or consultants in the field. (For the list of these leaders, see Appendix E.) In our interviews with these individuals, we focused on two basic questions.

- Do you think that strategic restructuring activity will increase, decrease, or remain the same in the nonprofit sector in the next 10 years? What is the basis for your prediction?
- If you feel that strategic restructuring activity will remain the same or increase, what do you think the impact of this activity will be on the nonprofit sector in the next 10 years?

In this chapter we discuss their answers to these questions.

Most of the leaders—17 out of 20—predicted that strategic restructuring would increase in the years to come, but their reasons varied. The majority linked growth in consolidation to changes in public policies that are intensifying competition in the nonprofit sector. Some pointed to policies designed to foster competition, such as vouchers for social services. Mark Rosenman, vice president at the Union Institute, Office for Social Responsibility, noted that the current interest among public agencies in giving clients vouchers to purchase services, rather than providing funds directly to organizations, may make it difficult for some organizations to persist. In such an environment, organizations may feel compelled to combine resources through strategic restructuring partnerships to competitively market their services to potential clients. Because vouchers make it difficult for organizations to predict revenue flows—funds come in sporadically as clients purchase services rather than at more predictable intervals from government contracts or grants—small organizations may look for capital through partnerships to tide them over during slow cash-flow periods. Rosenman's comments reflect the theory, discussed in chapter 2, that organizations structure themselves to increase or maintain revenue flows.

Government's interest in creating more of a marketplace mentality, in which competition increases quality and efficiency, is reflected not only in interest in vouchers but also in managed care strategies. In our conversations with leaders, several noted that government agencies are not implementing managed care principles as quickly as they expected—as evidenced in several of our case studies. However, these leaders believed that managed care would eventually have a significant impact, particularly on child welfare and mental health agencies. James Denova, a senior program officer at the Claude Worthington Benedum Foundation, has noticed many government funding streams shifting from making direct program grants to using managed care intermediaries.[1] To deal with such intermediaries, nonprofit managers must understand their cost structure, marketing, cash flow management, competition, and the benefits of cooperative ventures.

Other leaders saw competition rising because of the increase in the number of nonprofits rather than, or in addition to, a decrease in available funds. Sara Engelhardt, president of the Foundation Center, spoke of a proliferation of nonprofits during the recent economic boom. With the downturn in the economy in 2001/2002, which created more competition for resources, Engelhardt expected to see a consolidation trend over the next few years.

An increase in the number of competitors also may be an indirect effect of new government programs. Dorothy S. Ridings, president and CEO of the Council on Foundations, believes that the Bush administration's ongoing efforts to expand federal support for social services run by religious groups may lead to more faith-based institutions establishing separate 501(c)(3) organizations. This, she believes, will increase competition in the sector, and, in turn, increase consolidation. "I don't think that we can sustain the number of stand-alone nonprofits to the degree that the administration is looking at," said Ridings.

Another source of competition for nonprofits is for-profit companies. Lester Salamon, professor at the Institute for Policy Studies, Johns Hopkins University, and Elizabeth Boris, the director of the Center on Nonprofits and Philanthropy at the Urban Institute, both predict that government will (at least in the near future) continue to stress the involvement of the corporate sector in providing human services. To effectively compete with well-financed corporations, more nonprofits may combine their resources, and others may form partnerships with for-profits.

Competition was not the only reason the leaders predicted an increase in strategic restructuring activity. About a third believed that a rise in strategic restructuring would follow, at least in part, from funders pushing their grantees in this direction out of a belief that strategic restructuring can help organizations to be more cost effective. Sometimes the pressure is direct—funders suggest that organizations consolidate—and other times it is the result of changes in funder expectations, such as a requirement that grantees provide much more detailed accounting of how they used their funds and what outcomes they achieved. Such accounting requires computer systems that are too costly for many smaller organizations, so some may consolidate resources to purchase systems. Several leaders felt that funder's beliefs about the potential efficiencies gained through strategic restructuring might be misinformed and should be corrected or refined by research. This view of funders advocating for managerial strategies without a thorough understanding of their actual benefits reflects the portrayal of the nonprofit sector discussed earlier in the book. As noted in chapter 2, Paul DiMaggio and Walter Powell contend that, in the absence of clear indicators of organizational efficiency, funders sometimes reward certain organizational practices, which have gained popularity, even if there is no clear evidence that they are effective.

Another trend in the sector, venture philanthropy, addresses the interest in improving the efficiency of nonprofits by applying ideas and strategies of the for-profit world. Venture philanthropy is a term used to describe funders who, among other strategies, try to help their grantees improve their organizational capacity, much as venture capitalists do with the companies in which they invest. Ridings felt that venture philanthropists might cause more organizations to consider new ways to increase their income and to create synergies among organizations. However, Jeffrey Bradach, managing partner at the Bridgespan Group, expressed a cautionary note about the potential impact of venture philanthropists. More and more articles, books, and seminars on the topic have appeared in recent years, but if and when it will become a significant force is not clear. Bradach maintained that, for the time being, the rhetoric about venture philanthropy outpaces the reality.

In addition to competition for dollars, some of the leaders with whom we spoke forecasted heated competition for human resources. Elizabeth Skidmore, division director for the National Center for Consultation and Professional Development at the Child Welfare League of America, felt that the sector is experiencing a staffing crisis as well as increased competition for board members. Organizations not able to find the leaders and employees they need may, in increasing numbers, consider sharing staff and board members, much as some of the organizations in our case studies have done.

Finally, among the 17 leaders who predicted a rise in strategic restructuring, there were a few who spoke of larger shifts in the nonprofit sector and the communities it serves. Audrey R. Alvarado, executive director of the National Council of Nonprofit Associations, believes that the sector is going through a period of transition and self-reflection. She has seen a growing number of articles and conversations focused on defining the purpose and values of the sector for the future. She predicts that a new cadre of leaders, coming out of nonprofit management programs at universities, will bring new ideas to the sector. Increased strategic restructuring, in her view, may be the result of this renewal, because organizations may be willing to be more fluid and creative in how they approach their work.

James Denova spoke of a redistribution of low-income populations in the Pittsburgh area, with people moving from densely populated neighborhoods in the city to areas outside of the city. Such demographic shifts, in Denova's opinion, may require the nonprofits that serve low-income communities to form service networks, through strategic restructuring and other strategies, to move resources closer to the people who need them.

It is worth noting that only two of the leaders felt that strategic restructuring would increase in the nonprofit sector as a *direct* result of the popularity of consolidations in the for-profit sector. However, as discussed, more than a few felt that the increasing focus on businesslike practices in the nonprofit sector would create pressures that might lead some organizations to consolidate in pursuit of greater efficiency.

Several leaders believed that, although there would be an increase in strategic restructuring in the near future, it would not be a rapid one. Barbara Kibbe, director of the Organizational Effectiveness and Philanthropy program at the David and Lucile Packard Foundation, thought that, without a strong knowledge base about what works and what does not, strategic restructuring would increase at a slow pace. By contrast, Rosenman thought that emerging research in the area might moderate enthusiasm for strategic restructuring, particularly among those likely to pursue it as the latest management trend.

A few of the leaders we interviewed noted even stronger forces that would limit the number of strategic restructurings in the future. Boris maintains that funder and government interest in small, local, faith-based organizations may lead to the creation of more nonprofits serving niche populations rather than fewer, larger, consolidated, multiservice organizations. Similarly, Bradach notes that many funders are concerned about

supporting "local capacity." He, however, feels that such a bias may sometimes result in organizations operating at a subscale level, a size at which
they cannot make economies of scale work.

I don't know what the right number of organizations is for the sector . . . but it's
likely smaller than it is. Everything is so undercapitalized that if the capital were
allocated more effectively towards organizations that produce demonstrable results, we might see some larger scale organizations and more social impact.

While there are some good reasons for supporting small, local groups
(e.g., building social capital and strong communities), he feels most funders' dedication to relatively small grants and to small nonprofits may
prevent consolidation into fewer, larger groups.

Only three of the leaders with whom we spoke looked at the nonprofit
landscape and saw dwindling or steady rates of strategic restructuring.
William Ryan, a research fellow at the Hauser Center for Nonprofit Organizations at Harvard University, guessed that many of the organizations
that were most likely to try strategic restructuring (because of their belief
in its potential benefits, and/or high motivation levels stemming from
imminent threats to their organizations) have already tried it. He further
surmised that the small number of organizations that are prone to try
popular management strategies may have already moved on to other
strategies.

Interestingly, those who see strategic restructuring increasing and those
who do not both feel funder perspectives are at the root of strategic restructuring prevalence. Although some see funders pushing nonprofits,
either directly or indirectly, to consolidate, Christine Letts, a lecturer in
public policy and associate director at the Hauser Center, thought that
funder attitudes would keep the number of strategic restructuring partnerships down. In her opinion, many funders do not want to tip the scales
in favor of any particular organization to help it dominate the market.
She felt that this attitude was shortsighted and, like Bradach, thought that
funders should look at how their funding choices can help to increase
efficiency and performance in social service. Letts also felt that funders
are not interested in becoming involved in strategic restructuring, because
it focuses on general operating issues, which are difficult for them to sell
to their boards. She described funders as shying away from long-term
efforts like strategic restructuring in favor of supporting time-limited
projects.

In sum, although the 20 leaders were united neither in their predictions
about the future course of strategic restructuring in the nonprofit sector
nor in their views of what the factors affecting that course would be, most
saw consolidation as being on the rise, largely due to financial pressures.
In general, they felt such pressures were the result of increased competi-

tion for dollars as well as of changing policies and perspectives among public and private funders.

The leaders offered both positive and negative predictions about the potential impact of strategic restructuring on the sector. For example, six thought that strategic restructuring would lead to the provision of more and/or better services in the sector, and five expected that it would lead to greater efficiency in the sector. However, even these optimists were concerned about potential downsides and abuses of strategic restructuring. Audrey R. Alvarado, executive director of the National Council of Nonprofit Associations, predicted that, if organizations pursue strategic restructuring for the right reasons, the ultimate impact will be better services that are more in line with community and client needs. For example, if organizations look at families and communities with a holistic perspective, they may form service networks that provide continuums of care for clients. However, she also expressed concern that strategic restructuring partnerships designed solely for organizational survival, without consideration of the impact on clients, might undermine the missions of some organizations.

Running throughout our discussions with leaders was a debate over whether a smaller number of large nonprofits is better than a larger number of small ones. Most of the leaders seemed to agree that strategic restructuring favors fewer and larger organizations. Most also worried about what the loss of small organizations would mean.

"If it makes it harder for small, newer nonprofits to establish themselves and succeed, then it will really dampen innovation in the sector," said Benjamin Shute, secretary and treasurer of the Rockefeller Brothers Fund. Rosenman forecasted the same outcome because, in his opinion, larger organizations tend to become less creative institutions, choosing instead to "play things safer." Skidmore added that small organizations can be more nimble in responding to the market than larger ones. Shute felt that, if size leads to the "corporatization" of nonprofits, then this might, in turn, result in jeopardizing the tax exemption of some agencies, or in refocusing some human service organizations from their missions to efficiency pursuits such as skimming the easiest-to-serve clients and rationing services.

Another primary concern that arose in our discussions was that the trend toward strategic restructuring might reduce the number of organizations that focus on underserved communities. Consolidation, Skidmore explained, can lead to centralizing operations and closing community-based facilities. When organizations move, they sometimes lose board members and other volunteers who do not want to commute to the new location or who find that the organization is no longer focused on the community of concern to them. Skidmore also worried that strategic restructuring would reduce the number of minority-focused organizations. She has observed that when such groups partner with larger organizations they lose their individual character and mission focus. Virginia Hodgkin-son, Director of the Research Center for the Study of Voluntary Organi-zations and Public Service at Georgetown Public Policy Institute, added that small organizations—which often provide much-needed services not offered by larger ones—often do not have the resources needed to restruc-ture. She warned that, unless we help them to collaborate, we may lose many of them.

A smaller number of leaders thought bigger would be better. Letts, for example, predicted that, if the nonprofit sector included fewer and larger organizations, these organizations would have much greater influence with funders and have less of a supplicant relationship to them. Bradach, as noted, felt that strategic restructuring could help some organizations operate more efficiently, by bringing them to a size that would allow them to take advantage of economies of scale. Peter C. Brinckerhoff of Corporate Alternatives Inc., however, warned that size comes with certain costs. He suggested that funders encourage and fund capacity building because, if organizations are going to be larger, they will need larger and better-educated staffs, including more specialists such as HR, development, and IT professionals.

Three leaders questioned the conventional wisdom that strategic re-structuring will increase due to funders' concerns about duplication of services. Shute was not convinced that there is a large degree of dupli-cation within the nonprofit sector. Rather, he saw organizations approach-ing issues with different strategies and philosophies, so that, even though they may be addressing the same problem, they are providing different services. Similarly, Kibbe disagreed that the sector is overcrowded with organizations. She felt that a vital society depends on change in the sector, including the creation, dissolution, and restructuring of organizations to address changing needs, perspectives, and interests.

Perhaps the most dire warnings came from Salamon and Rosenman, who worried that strategic restructuring, along with other trends, would alter the nonprofit sector in fundamental ways. Salamon predicted that the increased commercialization of the sector (as a result of the changes in funding patterns) may alter its essential character, including its com-mitment to mission, values, advocacy, and quality over efficiency. Simi-larly, Rosenman felt that an increase in strategic restructuring would lead to a further erosion of the nonprofit sector's focus on mission, and the ascendancy of management, administration, and finance over program concerns.

The 20 leaders' perspectives, taken together, add up to both optimism and concern. Most saw strategic restructuring increasing in the years ahead due to changes in the way nonprofits are financed that, in turn, are the result of changes in the beliefs of funders about how organizations should operate and the role of competition within the nonprofit sector.

They generally thought that an increase in strategic restructuring could mean an increase in the efficient use of resources among nonprofits. However, many of them registered deep concern about potential harmful side effects—loss of niche organizations, innovation, and services to particular communities, and even loss of the essential character of the sector.

NOTE

1. Intermediaries are networks of human service organizations established to contract with the government, monitor client services, provide central intake, and refer clients to appropriate network affiliates.

CHAPTER 9

Conclusion

What do we know about strategic restructuring, and what does it mean for individual nonprofits considering, starting up, and nurturing strategic restructuring partnerships, as well as for those supporting such organizations with money and advice?

Strategic restructuring should not be undertaken lightly. Research shows that such consolidations involve significant investments of time, trust, and money. The benefits can equal or exceed the necessary costs under the right conditions. However, without careful planning and oversight, the opposite outcome is likely. In this final chapter we summarize some basic learning on strategic restructuring and make recommendations drawing on the findings from our research and that of others.

UNDER WHAT CONDITIONS DO ORGANIZATIONS CONSOLIDATE?

Most nonprofits that consider strategic restructuring do so when internal or external changes, current or projected, put a significant proportion of their operations in jeopardy, or threaten to make their operations gradually less efficient or relevant. Such changes include rising facilities costs, loss of resources, funding reforms (such as managed care), increased reporting requirements, and difficulty finding and keeping personnel. Some research suggests that nonprofits may successfully pursue strategic restructuring even without such threatening changes. For example, an organization may consider joint programming when it lacks some of the funding, facilities, expertise, personnel, or other resources needed to manage a particular program on its own. However, most of the research conducted so far shows nonprofits consolidating because of significant changes within and outside of their organizations. Table 9.1 lists the potential costs and benefits of each type of strategic restructuring partnership.

Table 9.1
Common Benefits and Costs and Challenges of Strategic Restructuring by Type of Partnership

POTENTIAL BENEFITS	JP*	AC	MSO	JV	PS	M
Organizational identity/brand name preserved	•	•	•	•	•	
Increased expertise in management of programming	•				•	•
New services/programs with relatively minor investment	•			•		
Positive PR due to association with partner(s)	•	•	•	•	•	•
Improved quality of administrative staff and services		•	•		•	•
Economies of scale in areas such as facilities, staff benefits, supplies, and technology		•	•		•	•
No need to set up and/or oversee a new organization	•	•				
Perceived independence of entity providing administrative services			•			
Shared liability for new and legally separate organization			•	•		
Clarity about which organization has ultimate authority					•	
Better market positioning	•	•	•	•	•	•
Easily understood both internally and externally						•
Although more upfront negotiation regarding roles, less ongoing negotiation						•

(continued)

Table 9.1
Continued

POTENTIAL COSTS/CHALLENGES	JP*	AC	MSO	JV	PS	M
Confusion among funders about who is in charge	•	•	•	•		
Time spent on coordination	•	•	•	•	•	
Differential investment by the organizations involved	•	•	•	•	•	
Negative PR due to association with partner(s)	•	•	•	•	•	•
Staff members, particularly senior managers, stretched to their limits		•	•	•	•	•
Difficulty in deciding when to expand administrative capacity		•	•		•	•
Difficulty in responding swiftly to idiosyncratic needs of affiliates			•			
Difficulties with cultural integration and differing expectations		•	•	•	•	•
Staff turnover (voluntary and involuntary)			•		•	•
Initiative becomes neglected stepchild of partner organizations	•			•		
Confusion regarding who is responsible for what		•	•	•	•	
Difficulties negotiating relationship between parent and subsidiar(y)(ies)—lack of clarity regarding whether subsidiaries are subordinates or customers					•	
Organizational identit(y)(ies)/brand name(s) lost						•
Time and money spent on integration of people and systems		•	•		•	•
Funders believing they can reduce their overall support once grantees are merged						•

*JP = Joint Programming; AC = Administrative Consolidation; MSO = Management Service Organization; JV = Joint Venture; PS = Parent-Subsidiary; M = Merger

WHAT ARE THE PRIMARY BENEFITS OF STRATEGIC RESTRUCTURING?

Organizations that form strategic restructuring partnerships may benefit from increased and improved public relations, access to greater administrative and/or programmatic expertise, and improved staff benefits. Public relations benefits grow from associations with partner organizations, from the appearance (and in some cases, the actuality) of operating more efficiently, and simply from being part of a larger entity that can more easily attract attention. Through such PR boosts, partnering organizations may be able to achieve greater recognition and eventually a larger market share. They may be better positioned to grow and move into new markets and to anticipate strategic opportunities and threats. Additionally, strategic restructuring allows organizations to pool resources to hire more experienced staff members and to benefit from the expertise of each partner's current employees. And economies of scale gained through strategic restructuring make it possible for organizations to buy better insurance plans for their employees; further, staff may feel that their jobs are more secure within a larger structure and may gain opportunities for advancement.

We need more in-depth research to understand the conditions under which organizations save money or increase revenues as a result of strategic restructuring. Our research shows that organizations can economize on facilities, staff benefits, supplies, and technology by consolidating. However, how these savings compare to the costs of strategic restructuring remains unclear. Also uncertain is whether and how savings persist over time.

Organizations involved in partnerships may have an edge over competitors because they offer a greater range of services or have stronger administrative infrastructures (especially in a managed care environment). Funders may favor such nonprofits because they perceive them to be more innovative and efficient. Thus strategic restructuring may lead to increased revenues for partner organizations. However, further examination of this issue must precede more definitive conclusions.

WHAT SHOULD THOSE PLANNING AND IMPLEMENTING STRATEGIC RESTRUCTURING LOOK OUT FOR?

Like any significant organizational reform, strategic restructuring requires strong leadership. A nonprofit that lacks leaders who already have the trust and support of most of their staff and board should carefully consider whether the organization can successfully weather—and benefit from—a partnership. An exception might be an organization where the leader is leaving or has departed, and which has had difficulty finding a strong successor. Under these conditions, strategic restructuring offers a way to take advantage of the leader(s) of another organization. However, to realize the goals it has set for strategic restructuring (such as maintaining service to a particular population or preserving a certain philosophy about how it does its work), such an organization still needs strong representation and guidance from its board and senior management.

Another important consideration for an organization considering strategic restructuring is whether it has sufficient resources, including both time and money, for planning and implementing a partnership. In addition to their everyday work, staff and board members will be called upon to participate in long meetings during the planning stages. Such meetings are likely to continue during implementation, and perhaps take even more time as additional staff members get into the nitty-gritty of hammering out policies and procedures. And, for most types of strategic restructuring, the need for increased communication—through meetings, newsletters, events, Web sites, and E-mails—will continue. Successfully working across organizations requires a significant investment in sharing information and building consensus in order to ensure that the right hand is up-to-date on the workings of the left hand, that operations are efficient and well-coordinated, that opportunities are not missed, that cultures blend (at least in part) and, perhaps most important, that misinformation does not spread and undermine the partnership.

Strategic restructuring also entails out-of-pocket costs. Initially, there may be attorneys to hire and facilities and refreshment expenses for meetings and other gatherings. As the partnership progresses, additional staff such as HR and communications professionals may be needed. Moreover, although some staff (particularly senior staff and middle managers) can, at least in theory, attend to partnership responsibilities without neglecting their regular jobs, some programs and operations may suffer if organizations do not hire new staff or restructure staffing to prevent such neglect.

Another potential financial cost of strategic restructuring is a consultant fee. Only two of the six cases that we examined used consultants, and only one used a consultant with expertise in strategic restructuring. Given the limited use of consultants in the case studies, our conclusions on this point are based on only a few observations. It appears that simple partnerships, such as joint programming or limited administrative consolidations, are relatively easy to handle without a consultant, assuming that the organizations involved have strong leadership and sufficient resources. However, several of those we spoke with in the more complex consolidations, particularly the joint venture and merger cases, felt that their partnerships would have benefited from a consultant with strategic restructuring expertise. They felt that they needed someone who could help them set realistic expectations, point out potential pitfalls, and offer advice about how to optimize success. Perhaps even more important, they felt a neutral party might have helped them avoid or better deal with stalemates in negotiations.[1]

By contrast, the director of the parent organization in our parent-subsidiary case—perhaps the most complex partnership in our sample—believed that the partners made it through the planning and implementation stages fairly successfully without a consultant. He attributed their success to having a clear and widely supported goal for the partnership, a goal that they refocused on whenever they ran into trouble.

WHAT SHOULD THOSE PLANNING AND IMPLEMENTING STRATEGIC RESTRUCTURING DO TO OPTIMIZE SUCCESS?

An organization can stack the odds in its favor if it chooses a partner that many or most people in the organization know and respect. Because trust and communication are vital to making consolidations work, a partnership benefits from not having to start from scratch—teaching one another about the organizations' work, getting to know one another. However, organizations should not assume that they know their partners well enough to completely skip such activities. As the merger case demonstrated, just because organizations are similar to and familiar with each other in some ways does not mean that there will not be areas of significant contrast and divergence. Assumptions (both positive and negative) about partners can impede the strategic restructuring process by creating false or unreasonable expectations and by blinding partners to potential time bombs and opportunities. So it is important to find reasonable partners and then get to know them even better.

Our case studies also show the importance of setting realistic expectations. This can be difficult, and even painful, in the short run. Some leaders want to reassure their staffs that strategic restructuring will not result in significant changes. In some partnerships and for some staff members, this reassuring prospect may be the case. However, knowing to the greatest extent possible how the partnership will proceed, what the stages are, how quickly it will progress, and how it will change operations, jobs, facilities, and so on, in both the short term and the long term, helps to dispel fears and prepare staff for the partnership process. Some will decide to opt out. Others will be pleased by the changes. Many will be skeptical or hesitant. This latter group may be reassured when they see the partnership proceeding as predicted, and appreciate the relationship between interim steps and ultimate goals.

Of course, no partnership, no matter how well planned and informed by research, can predict its exact course. So one of the most important expectations leaders can set at the outset is that those involved will face *unexpected* challenges along the way. Leaders may also outline how such challenges will be handled. For example, what committees and/or individuals should be notified of unexpected challenges, what group or person will work to resolve them, and how will this group or individual go about doing so?

An important tool for setting expectations is an internal communications plan. Some combination of organizational newsletters, internal Web sites, staff meetings, special gatherings, and one-on-one discussions can comprise a plan to keep staff members informed, and give them forums to discuss and make suggestions as the planning and implementation stages progress. A public relations strategy is also important to keep key constituencies—clients, funders, public officials, community members, regulating bodies, and the like—up to date on the partnership and how it will affect their relationships with the organizations involved.

Another important tool is an implementation plan. Without a guide to how and what needs to be integrated, many strategic restructuring partnerships will stall after negotiations, with the parties tired out and ready to move on. Good implementation planning should begin even before the deal is set, and a clear timeline and defined role for each participant is essential. Part of the implementation plan should also be a statement of the desired outcomes for the strategic restructuring, so that the outcomes can later be evaluated.

RECOMMENDATIONS FOR FUTURE STRATEGIC RESTRUCTURING RESEARCH

Although our study and others provide important information for those considering and planning strategic restructuring, we still have much to learn. To chart out the next round of research, we asked the 20 leaders in the nonprofit and philanthropic sectors whom we interviewed what additional knowledge about strategic restructuring would be helpful to nonprofit managers, funders, board members, and consultants. We conclude with their answers.

A more detailed understanding of the costs and benefits of strategic restructuring would help everyone considering strategic restructuring (8 out of 20 leaders).

- How much does it cost to complete various types of strategic restructuring?
- What are the short-term versus long-term costs and benefits of strategic restructuring partnerships? Do they save money in the long term?
- How do the benefits attributable to strategic restructuring compare to other efforts to realize similar benefits?

- How does strategic restructuring affect organizational missions?
- When does the ethic of expense reduction become too stringent and hamper the health of an organization?

More case studies would also inform strategic restructuring decisions. (6 out of 20 leaders)

- What can be learned from cases that were particularly successful or particularly problematic?
- What is the status of the partnerships profiled in the case studies conducted for Phase II, three years after the study? How have these strategic restructuring partnerships affected clientele composition, revenue streams, and perception of service in the communities served by the partner organizations?

A broad examination of the impact of strategic restructuring on the nonprofit sector would be helpful, particularly to funders (6 out of 20 leaders).

- What are the nonmonetary, broader costs of strategic restructuring, such as loss of pluralism?
- Is a strategic restructuring trend limiting our ability to service certain communities? (Indicators might include the number of residential treatment beds and foster care homes that are available versus the demand.)
- Has strategic restructuring helped the nonprofit sector to better position itself for advocacy efforts?

Investigation of partnership life cycles would provide information to guide planning (6 out of 20 leaders).

- What are the life cycles of various types of partnerships? Do partnerships that begin by sharing a limited number of administrative functions often develop into more integrated partnerships? In other words, is an alliance the first step toward merger?
- What happens after the marriage? How can organizations best deal with the cultural integration challenges that occur after a partnership/merger is established?
- What are the continuing effects of consolidations that began many years ago?

Exploration of funders' roles in strategic restructuring would inform future funding decisions regarding strategic restructuring (4 out of 20 leaders).

- To what extent have funders been willing to pay for strategic restructuring?
- How has funders' support of consolidated organizations changed over time?
- Is there a relationship between organizations' primary income sources (earned

income, government funding, private funding, etc.) and the organizations' level of strategic restructuring activity?

We began this book describing the perspective of some people in the nonprofit sector who believe in the common sense or inevitability of consolidation among organizations. We hope that by investigating fundamental questions about the operation and funding of nonprofits, by reviewing relevant research, and, perhaps most important, by looking closely at the experience of organizations that have tried various types of partnerships, we have offered a more thorough and nuanced understanding of strategic restructuring.

NOTE

1. One of the author's own consulting experience with dozens of strategic restructuring processes suggests that this last may be the most important contribution a consultant can make.

APPENDIX A

Case Study Stories

JOINT PROGRAMMING: SPOKANE COUNTY MICROENTERPRISE DEVELOPMENT PROGRAM

OVERVIEW OF PARTNERSHIP

Spokane Neighborhood Action Program, a human service organization with a wide range of programs for low-income residents of Spokane, Washington, formed a micro-enterprise program with Northwest Business Development Association, which provides loans to small businesses in the Spokane area. The two organizations jointly run the program, which recruits, educates, and provides loans to low-income adults interested in starting small businesses. Outside of the micro-enterprise program, the two organizations function independently. (See Table A.1.)

Whom We Interviewed

Ray Lancaster
Microenterprise Specialist
Spokane Neighborhood Action Programs

Carla Preston
Business Development Specialist
Small Business Development Center

Allen Schmelzer
Board Member
Northwest Business Development Association

Table A.1
Joint Programming Partnership

The Partners	Spokane Neighborhood Action Programs (SNAP)	Northwest Business Development Association (NWBDA)
Location	Spokane, Washington	Spokane, Washington
Program Focus	Multiple services including human services, housing, and economic opportunities	Loans to small businesses
Founded	1985	1982
Approximate Annual Budget	$9 million	$600,000
Number of Full-Time Equivalent Staff	129	6

Larry Stuckart
Executive Director
Spokane Neighborhood Action Programs

Renee Warner
Business Development Officer
Northwest Business Development Association

Gary Whelpley
President
Northwest Business Development Association

The Story of the Partnership

Spokane Neighborhood Action Programs (SNAP) was established to improve the lives of the working poor, low-income elderly, families living in poverty, and the homeless of Spokane, Washington. It has pursued this through a wide range of services, such as emergency assistance and housing programs. But in 1997 it was looking for long-term solutions for eliminating poverty in the lives of its clients. Its leaders knew the solution must involve employment, but they had little expertise in this area. So, they called a meeting of those in the community who did: the Northwest Business Development Association, the Business Information

Center at the Chamber of Commerce, and the City of Spokane's Community Development Department. The meeting had only a vague agenda, to explore ways to employ low-income residents of Spokane. SNAP was experienced in working with other organizations, but usually with others in the human services world. Interacting with those in business and economic development was a relatively new experience.

The representatives from the institutions got to know each other through a series of meetings during the year. Eventually they began to see that by drawing on their collective skills and interests they could develop a program that would help low-income residents start their own businesses. Such a program appealed to those in the group who wanted to spur economic development in Spokane, and to SNAP's interest in economic opportunities for the poor. Larry Stuckart, executive director of SNAP, recalled that in the face of the needs in the community, what the representatives called a "microenterprise program" felt like a piece of work they could reasonably bite off.

The next step was to find money for the program. SNAP pursued its usual sources of grant funds, some local and some national. It was able to raise enough money from foundations, government, and some local banks to cover the salary of a coordinator, but still needed money for a loan pool. Eventually someone in the group let SNAP know that one organization in the group had some extra money in the bank. "We became aware that . . . NWBDA (Northwest Business Development Association) is . . . a very successful not-for-profit, and in fact had funds that they could use for this," said Ray Lancaster, the SNAP staff member who would become the coordinator of the joint program.

NWBDA had a mandate from its board of directors to use excess funds generated from bond payments to help individuals with social or personal credit problems to start businesses. But its leaders knew that they would not able to do all the work necessary to meet these goals without making significant and costly changes in their operations. So they were interested in how a partnership might help.

As the micro-enterprise program idea developed, it became clear that NWBDA and SNAP had different but complementary areas of expertise. NWBDA did not have the time or know-how to do the business development education and post-lending assistance that would be necessary for low-income borrowers; SNAP did. SNAP did not have the funds or knowledge to make loans; NWBDA did. Moreover, even if SNAP could both make and monitor the loans, Lancaster said, it wouldn't. He felt that the separation of the capital side and social service side was critical, because SNAP, unlike NWBDA, became too close to clients to enforce compliance with a loan agreement. In other words, it would help to have one organization play good cop, and the other, if necessary, bad cop.

SNAP and NWBDA developed a policies and procedures manual for the program and asked the city of Spokane's Community Development Office to refer clients and the local Small Business Development Center (SBDC) to help with prescreening and post-loan support. (Representatives from both groups sit on the loan review board with staff from the two primary partners, but SNAP and NWBDA have the primary responsibility for the program.)

The only significant bump in the road came when, after a year of planning, creating brochures, and gearing up for the start date, the NWBDA board let their director go. "He had not informed their board very much about his involvement, and so it got a little dicey there," recalled Lancaster, "So I got invited to an emergency board meeting because they saw their name on this brochure and wondered what was going on. And I informed them that their past president had been involved in the planning for this. I had minutes and agendas of his involvement. And at this point they said that they would be able to fund the capital pool for the program."

The partnership began in the summer of 1998, and it makes loans of $65,000 per year in amounts of $1,000 to $10,000. Typically, a low-income person learns about the program from a social service professional and contacts SNAP to inquire about it. After assessing the person's needs, SNAP may refer him or her to the Small Business Center for a class on business development. The SNAP staff then augments that learning by reviewing materials presented at the class with the participant to make the material more relevant to his or her specific business ideas. SNAP then helps the client to think through financing options, including the costs and benefits of going to a family member, bank, or the organization's own loan program. If the person chooses the latter, the loan committee reviews the application. If approved, SNAP provides ongoing advice to the recipient while NWBDA makes the payments and enforces the terms of the loan.

The fairly small program does not have a dramatic effect on the organizations involved. The only significant costs of the program, according to most of those interviewed, are the SNAP coordinator's salary (which is financed through grants), and the losses on loans, which thus far have been within expectations for this type of program.

The program does eat up time, however. Staff at NWBDA and the Small Business Center spoke about the program adding to their already full-time duties but also stressed that they believed in the importance of the program and enjoyed the opportunity to work with a different type of clientele. Lancaster emphasized that making the program run smoothly requires a significant amount of relationship building and maintenance among staff at the different organizations, and that he spends a great deal of time on these issues.

The primary outcome of these efforts has been an increased range of services available to SNAP clients, including access to capital and business education. And NWBDA and SBDC have expanded their markets to include low-income individuals.

The staff at both organizations are quite happy with the program, and most foresaw relatively minor adjustments to the program in the future. For example, Gary Whelpley, president of NWBDA, would like to see the city and neighborhood groups more involved in making referrals to the program, to diversify the clientele; at the time of these interviews, no minorities or women were involved. Several of those interviewed spoke about increasing the size of the program's loan portfolio and the geographic focus of the program.

Stuckart and Lancaster both wondered whether the program might work better someday if SNAP were itself able to develop and manage a loan pool. Stuckart thought that, if SNAP ran the whole program, the process might be easier and faster for clients and perhaps result in more loans. Lancaster wondered if an in-house capital pool might, at some point, provide income for the program. However, Stuckart was unsure if SNAP could ever develop sufficient resources, systems, and expertise to track and police loans. Moreover, Lancaster maintained that the separation of social service and underwriting is very important to the effectiveness of the program.

So, in the interest of effectiveness and efficiency, SNAP and NWBDA have decided to continue to make the relatively minor investments necessary to make the program work—having staff work a little overtime, raising grant funds for the coordinator, and finding time for loan review meetings. If the partners did not work together, the program—and thus a growing number of small local businesses—probably would not exist.

THE STEPS–EVERY WOMAN'S HOUSE CASE

Overview of Partnership

STEPS (Substance Abuse, Treatment, Education, and Prevention Services) at Liberty Center, Inc. and Every Woman's House, Inc., a shelter for abused women, conducted a joint capital campaign and now jointly own the building that houses their offices in Wooster, Ohio. The two organizations also share some office equipment and several administrative staff, including an executive director. Their programs, however, operate independently. (See Table A.2.)

Table A.2
Administrative Consolidation Partnership

The Partners	STEPS (Substance Abuse Treatment, Education, and Prevention Services) formerly: Wayne County Alcoholism Services	Every Woman's House
Location	Wooster, Ohio	Wooster, Ohio
Program Focus	Substance abuse services	Shelter for abused women
Founded	1974	1979
Approximate Annual Budget	$1.7 million	$1 million
Number of Full-Time Equivalent Staff	40	20

Whom We Interviewed

Ashley Belden
Neighborhood Outreach Specialist
STEPS

Tammy J. Brooks
Former Executive Director
Every Woman's House

Bobbi Douglas
Executive Director
STEPS and EWH

Lara Ginsburg
Operations Director
STEPS

Mac Hawkins
Finance Director
Every Woman's House

Ronald E. Holtman
Board Member
STEPS

John W. Kropf
Board Member
Every Woman's House

Brenda P. Linnick
Executive Director
United Way of Wayne & Holmes Counties, Inc.

Sharon Nissley
Domestic Violence Advocate
Every Woman's House

Stephen Shapiro
Board Member
STEPS

Beverly Zemrock
Board Member
Every Woman's House

The Story of the Partnership

In the small town of Wooster, Ohio, population 26,000, many residents contribute annually to local social service agencies. In 1994, the local women's shelter, called "Every Woman's House" (EWH), was considering asking contributors to be even more generous so that EWH could buy a new facility.

Another agency in town, then called "Wayne County Alcoholism Services" (WCAS), was also bursting at the seams and coming to the end of its lease. And it too was planning a capital campaign. After a good deal of searching, it found an old factory building then being used by a local moving company in a part of town close to its clients and the other services and businesses these clients used. But the structure was too big and expensive for the agency. So it decided to look for another agency that might want to join it in purchasing the building.

The two organizations were not exactly competitors. Although some women in the shelter struggled with addictions, and some of the abusers were clients of WCAS, the organizations generally worked in different worlds, offering different types of support based on the differences in their clientele.

However, they lived in the same fundraising world. Wooster (and the surrounding area) is small enough that some of the board members for the two agencies knew each other. In fact, two were married to each other. Moreover, Bobbi Douglas, executive director of WCAS, and Tammy Brooks, executive director of EWH, were close friends. When they got together and discussed their respective organizations' plans for raising money, they realized that it would be difficult to compete for donations. So they started talking about running a campaign together, sharing the costs of purchasing and renovating the warehouse, and moving in together.

"The reason we thought it would work out financially was that Every Woman's House had very poor cash flow, but (WCAS) was rich in cash flow and monthly revenue," recalled Brooks.

Every Woman's House had a sizable chunk of reserves because we had a large contributor who gave us a lot of money throughout the year. WCAS had no money in reserves. We knew the risk to us was in fronting all of the initial start-up money, but we told WCAS they would have to carry us if we ran into cash-flow problems. The risk was we're going to drain all of our money, and we're going to trust you. We had to trust them at their word. There would be large financial losses for everyone involved if this arrangement didn't work out.

EWH had, over the course of its 15-year history, developed a devoted cadre of individual donors, while WCAS, which was larger and had a stronger administrative structure, appealed more to corporate funders. Brooks and Douglas hoped that, with these complimentary assets and by sharing overhead costs, they could not only avoid competing with each other, but also be able to purchase facilities that would be beyond each of their means if they did it on their own.

Their boards hoped so, too, but also had some concerns. The members of the EWH board, in particular, were worried that their agency, begun by a small group of local women, would lose its special focus on abused women and be swallowed up by the larger WCAS. Some board members felt that being associated with a substance abuse organization would hurt the popularity of their cause. According to this argument, victims of domestic violence evoked the sympathy of the community while substance abusers often were blamed for their troubles. These worries sparked debate at EWH board meetings.

Other concerns remained latent, according to one board member. The alliance

The boards spent a great deal of time hammering out what they would share in the new building and how they would share it. These discussions would sometimes grow tense, but eventually they worked out a complex but mutually satisfying series of solutions. For example, there are more STEPS staff members in the building, so the front receptionist's salary is split two-thirds–one-third. Other costs are split fifty-fifty, and still others are based on square footage. Although sharing the costs appears to have saved both organizations money, there have been some unexpected new expenses associated with living in a larger, better-equipped facility. The organizations discovered, for example, that they needed an operations director to deal with facilities issues. And indeed, EWH's rental costs have increased significantly, although STEPS's initially remained about the same.

Today EWH and STEPS share some administrative staff, facilities, and equipment, and coordinate some programs. All shared expenses covered by one organization are charged, on a per usage basis, to the other organization. The building also has some additional rental space that, when leased, is designed to reduce costs for both agencies. At the time of the case study, they were having trouble leasing the space, because, in Douglas's opinion, most organizations are not oriented toward sharing space and equipment. STEPS and EWH were also considering using the extra space to expand their programs.

Since moving in together, the organizations have found other ways to save money together. When STEPS's finance director left in 1998, the organization hired one highly experienced fiscal director and a bookkeeper, both of whom work part-time, on a contractual basis, for EWH. This change saved the organizations $12,000.

EWH benefits from receiving some staff support, such as 30 percent of the operations director's time, at no cost. Indeed, at the time of our interviews the administrators who worked across both organizations—the executive director, the operations director, and the finance director—appeared to be stretched to their limits, both because of the partnership and because STEPS had grown considerably in the prior few years. The organizations thus were working on determining a reasonable *and* economic staffing structure for the partnership.

Cost analyses have not been conducted, but the individuals with whom we spoke generally felt that the partnership had a positive net effect on their budgets. Moreover, both organizations have benefited in unexpected ways from the partnership. STEPS raised $4,000 from a mail solicitation conducted for EWH, because several donors sent checks for both organizations. Indeed, STEPS benefits in a number of ways from the public sympathy EWH generates. EWH, for example, draws more in-kind donations and volunteers than it needs, and passes along the excess to STEPS. Additionally, the partnership itself has been a source of good PR, according to interviewees. Donors seem to like the idea that the organizations are saving funds by sharing costs.

The clientele of both organizations seem to like the new facilities and location. Concerns that the safety of the women in the shelter might be compromised by the proximity to spaces where substance abusers—some of them also domestic abusers—receive services have not been borne out. On the whole, the partnership, according to most we interviewed, is invisible to clients.

A question in the back of some staff and board members' minds is whether the organizations will continue to consolidate functions until they completely merge. Four of the people we spoke with predicted that this would not occur. Two felt there was no need for this because the organizations do not compete for funds and run efficiently as they are. Five stressed that a merger would threaten the identities of the organizations, and in turn, jeopardize the interest of clients and funders who identify with one mission or the other.

Three people felt that a merger might be in the future. For example, if one organization were to lose significant funding, the other would be the logical organization to pick up its services. Lara Ginsburg, operations director for STEPS, felt that it may be time to look at the growth of both organizations and assess if the partnership is benefiting both sides. She thought they should consider ending the partnership or adding more administrative support to STEPS, given its growth. Looking at the three-year plan for STEPS, she saw the need for significant administrative support (to bring in more corporate funders and reduce reliance on government funds), and wondered whether this would be possible with some administrative staff splitting their time between the two organizations.

Another question is what to do when Douglas leaves. The boards recognize that it takes a unique combination of skills and traits to run two organizations. Steve Shapiro, a STEPS board member, felt that it would be difficult for a new director to learn the work of both organizations simultaneously, as well as learn the differences in cultures and approaches with clients. He thought that, although the decision to share a director had benefits in the shorter term, it may make things more difficult down the road. Others wondered whether the partnership would still work if each organization had its own director again.

Most of the people we interviewed, however, saw the relationship between the organizations continuing and growing. Some felt that more administrative functions should be shared, and some were interested in exploring programmatic collaborations. Douglas and the finance director, Mac Hawkins, both spoke about the potential benefits of the partnership transforming into a management service organization (MSO). Hawkins envisioned making all of the administrative staff employees of Community Crossroads and including administrative services costs in the rent for both agencies. He and Douglas saw a potential revenue generator in such an MSO. "If you set it up right, there's a lot of tiny little nonprofits in this community that could use payroll services, marketing services, whatever it might be," remarked Douglas.

This is a long-term goal, but the partners are already testing the waters by helping other local organizations—including their competitors—to use the new computer system required by the mental health boards. Hawkins noted that they are not charging for these services, just using the experiment as an opportunity to get to know the organizations and hoping it will pay dividends down the road.

Such a mindset has fueled the partnership since the beginning—looking for ways to make better use of resources and to avoid competition. Although counterintuitive for some staff and board members at points throughout the partnership's history, this strategy appears to have gradually taken root and changed the way the organizations operate.

PARTNERS FOR COMMUNITY

Overview of Partnership

Corporation for Public Management and New England Farm Workers' Council, both multipurpose human service organizations based in Springfield, Massachusetts, serving Massachusetts, Connecticut, southeastern New York, and southern New Hampshire, established a new organization, Partners for Community (PfC), to provide administrative support for their agencies. (See Table A.3.)

Whom We Interviewed

Jim Asselin
Executive Director
Hampden County Employment and Training Consortium[1]

Lillian Cruz
Executive Director
Humanidad Incorporated (PfC affiliate)

David Eve
Vice President, Information and Technology
Partners for Community

Table A.3
Management Service Organization Partnership

The Partners	Corporation for Public Management (CPM)	New England Farm Workers' Council (NEFWC)
Location	Springfield, Massachusetts	Springfield, Massachusetts
Program Focus	Human services, multipurpose	Human services, multipurpose
Founded	1982	1971
Approximate Annual Budget	$11.5 million	$30 million
Number of Full-Time Equivalent Staff	222	103

Heriberto Flores
Chairman
Partners for Community
(and Executive Director of New England Farm Workers' Council)

David Gadaire
Executive Director
CareerPoint (PfC affiliate)

Jeffrey Greim
Chief Operating Officer
Partners for Community

Carmen Luz
Program Director
New England Farm Workers' Council

Jane Malone
Vice President for Administration
Partners for Community

Lorraine Montalto
Program Director
Corporation for Public Management

Bill Persch
Director, Marketing
Partners for Community

Jerome L. Weiner
President/CEO
Partners for Community
(and President of Corporation for Public Management)

The Story of the Partnership

The board of Corporation for Public Management (CPM) and its president, Jerome Weiner, looked at the organization's revenues and expenses in the mid-1990s and did not know how they were going to make the math work in the years ahead. For income, they mostly relied on contracts with government agencies. These contracts had not grown at even the cost of living over the prior few years. CPM had to either cut back or find a new way to cover the costs of running its programs.

Around the same time, it was becoming clear to Heriberto Flores that he and his organization, New England Farm Workers Council (NEFWC), were stretched to the limit despite their success in winning grants and contracts. Flores, who was the first Latino appointed to the board of the University of Massachusetts and who served on the New England Community Development Advisory Council of the Federal Reserve Bank of Boston, was spending an increasing amount of time on external relations. This was time well spent, since it seemed to be resulting in more grants for his agency. But it also left him with less time for daily management, and the growth of NEFWC created a lot more paperwork, which was taxing his administrative staff. Moreover, many of NEFWC's government grants are "pass through," providing little or no provision for overhead expenses associated with administrating the programs funded.

With these concerns in mind, Flores called his long-time friend Weiner in 1996, and asked if CPM would consider merging with NEFWC. When asked if the notion frightened him, Weiner responded, "No, I wished I had thought of it. It was scarier to think of what the future of CPM might be without some significant changes."

Some of the benefits were clear right away. Both Flores and Weiner believed that public agencies were looking to manage fewer contracts and to only deal with larger organizations that could provide a range of services. By consolidating, they could do just that. Plus, their strengths seemed to complement each other. Flores brought his political acumen and contacts. Weiner brought strong management skills and an experienced administrative team.

Their talks continued, but they ruled out a full-scale merger fairly quickly. Attorneys and funding sources advised them that a merger might necessitate rebidding on, and thus possibly losing, government contracts that did not allow the transference of funds from one organization to another. Additionally, neither organization wanted to jeopardize the good reputation associated with its name. Weiner proposed the MSO structure after researching its use in the health care field.

An MSO was appealing not only because it allowed both organizations to maintain their identities and a fair amount of autonomy, but also because it seemed less complex and safer than a merger. "It's something you can walk away from," noted Weiner. Additionally, the MSO form provided a relatively easy way for other organizations to join them, thus increasing the human and financial resources available to all the partners. At the same time, like a merger, it allowed them to combine resources to develop a stronger administrative infrastructure with higher quality fiscal, human resource, and technological systems and staff.

Weiner, knowing that ego issues among board members can kill merger and affiliation talks, was concerned about how the two boards might react to the idea. He was surprised and reassured at a joint meeting of the boards when several CPM board members knew NEFWC members. Moreover, no one seemed to feel threatened by the idea, because the MSO would leave both boards intact.

Many meetings with funders, policymakers, and other stakeholders followed. Most agreed the MSO was the way to go. Jim Asselin, of the Hampden County Employment and Training Consortium, admitted that the proportion of the Consortium's grants that it allowed grantees to use for administration (3 to 5 percent) was "obscenely small," and thought that the MSO was a good way for organizations to stretch administrative dollars. He also hoped that the MSO could help maintain administrative quality and management stability for the organizations involved, some of which had experienced a great deal of turnover, especially among finance staff.

Weiner and Flores easily determined their respective roles in the MSO, which was to be called Partners for Community (PfC). Because Flores had strong political credentials in the community, he became the chair of PfC, focusing on public relations work. Given his interest and strength in operations, Weiner serves as president and chief executive. Although a staffing chart would show Weiner reporting to Flores, they essentially work as partners.

To announce the new structure to their staffs, Weiner and Flores rented three rooms in a hotel. First, the staffs met separately with their own directors and were given time to ask questions. Then both staffs met in a large ballroom along with a consultant with expertise in nonprofit mergers and alliances. Reactions were mixed. Some were relieved that the plan was to grow rather than contract, but others—especially middle and senior management, whose jobs were most vulnerable to economies-of-scale measures—expressed fears of a future merger and loss of jobs and influence within the MSO structure.

Weiner and Flores followed the big announcement with a series of meetings and one-on-one discussions to answer questions about how the changes would affect particular positions. "We wanted to make certain that individuals felt a stake in the MSO," recalls Flores.

At the beginning, Weiner and Flores vowed that there would be no layoffs, and struggled to keep the promise by helping some staff to adjust to new positions needed for the new structure. A few had trouble with the transition and left their jobs, including a fiscal officer whose position was made obsolete by the MSO.

The first savings came when CPM moved into the same building with NEFWC, in November 1996. The physical proximity of staff also helped to unify the staff operationally and psychologically. In 1998, they purchased an adjacent building, where the programs of both organizations are located.

Another action the organizations took early on was to hire Jeff Greim as the chief operating officer for PfC. Since then, he has overseen the transfer of all of the financial information to one accounting program, and has reorganized the flow of work so that the financial staff work according to function rather than agency. The larger perspective and impartiality of an outside person was critical to the integration process, according to Jane Malone, PfC's vice president of administration. Greim admits that he wrestles with how much he should push staff to adapt to new roles. "It's a balance between gutting what you have in order to make room for something new or allowing what you have to evolve into what you want it to become," says Greim. "We have chosen to stress evolution," he adds.

One of the most significant challenges came when they applied for 501(c)(3) tax status for PfC. They wanted to make sure that no one questioned the nonprofit status of any affiliate, and they worried this might happen if PfC were not a nonprofit. The IRS ruled that, as a nonprofit, PfC would be competing with for-profits that did not have the tax advantage that it did, and so denied it 501(c)(3) status. After speaking with their legal advisors, the organizations made the unusual decision to appeal the IRS ruling. After two years of going back and forth, making presentations, and asking for more information, the IRS granted the 501(c)(3), and made it retroactive to the first day that PfC was formed.

In 1997, the International Language Institute of Massachusetts, a language education center, joined PfC; and in 1998 Brightwood Development Corporation, a small community development corporation, became an affiliate. The most recent affiliates are CareerPoint, an employment-training center, and Humanidad, which provides culturally sensitive housing services for mentally disabled individuals in the Hartford, Connecticut, Latino community. To become an affiliate, an organization must be incorporated as a nonprofit under section 501(c)(3) of the U.S. tax code, sign a confidentiality agreement, and cooperate with a due diligence process focused on fiscal issues. The next step is to sign an affiliation agreement that enumerates the responsibilities of the affiliate and of PfC.

The MSO services that each organization uses are described in Table A.4. All of the current affiliates are organizations that Weiner or Flores had some type of relationship with previously and that provide services of use to clients of CPM or NEFWC. PfC, still in the developmental phase, has decided to bring on affiliates and charge them minor or no fees to build relationships that help PfC to develop a continuum of care and that may become more integrated in the future.

As planned, all affiliates have gained from being part of a larger entity. "Improving our information technology was reason enough for us to come together," claims Weiner.

To develop and maintain the computer systems needed for financial management and program tracking, you either have to make a large capital investment or enter into a long-term lease, and both sap resources. Economies of scale really make sense in this area.

The half million dollars PfC has invested in technology helps the affiliates on a

Table A.4
Partners for Community Affiliates

Affiliate	Program Focus	MSO Service Used	Cost of MSO Services
Corporation for Public Management	Employment and other human services	All administrative support functions	CPM transfers all funds raised for overhead expenses to PfC
New England Farm Workers' Council	Employment, day care, fuel assistance, and other services for Latino families	All administrative support functions	NEFWC transfers all funds raised for overhead expenses to PfC
Brightwood Development Corporation	Community development corporation	All administrative support functions	No charge
International Language Institute of Massachusetts	Language Instruction	Human resources services	No charge
CareerPoint	Employment workforce development	Sharing information/ access to community leaders	Minor annual fee
Humanidad	Housing for mentally disabled Latino clients	Fiscal, HR, IT, program development	Monthly flat fee

number of fronts. It allows them to track clients and provide funders with information on their progress. The new computer systems also make it possible to run more sophisticated financial programs, to communicate more effectively among the 350 employees of the affiliates, and to communicate with the outside world through a consolidated Web site.

The MSO also provides a way to respond to two primary, seemingly contradictory, concerns of public funders. On the one hand, government agencies find it easier to provide a few major grants to large organizations rather than to oversee many smaller grants to grassroots agencies. On the other hand, the agencies are interested in community-based approaches to human service needs. PfC can address both concerns.

Another key benefit, according to Weiner, has been his partnership with Flores. "An executive director often gets filtered information from his or her staff. Now I have someone to bounce ideas off of, someone to challenge me. . . . A partner is a better thing to have than a competitor." Staff benefits have improved as a result of the MSO, as well. In addition to making it possible to purchase better and more insurance because of increased size and resources, the creation of the MSO has given some employees more potential for growth within the organization. And PfC was able to save CPM and NEFWC money by reducing the number of staff in the fiscal, administrative, and technology areas, enabling bulk purchasing in technology hardware and software, and facilitating the sharing of office space and phone lines.

The effect on services is less clear. The PfC leaders hope that by providing a "single point of entry" for services at all of the affiliate agencies, they will enable clients to access and move among services more easily. They also hope that the increased amount of training they are able to provide for staff as a result of the consolidation will improve services.

The directors of two affiliates stress the political benefits of their relationship with PfC. Lillian Cruz, executive director of Humanidad, felt that when the organization operated on its own, it was able to provide services at low cost. Their funders, however, were sending signals that they did not want to deal with agencies with smaller budgets. David Gadaire, executive director of CareerPoint, said that his organization's primary interest in joining PfC was the influence with funders and elected officials that would be gained through the association. "There is lots of turfism, lots of politics, in this area, and you want to make sure you are on the right team," noted Gadaire.

The MSO has confused some in the broader community as well as some who work for the agencies. Although a front-page article in the local paper helped to clarify the structure, many continue to view it as a merger. PfC has worked to explain its function through newsletters, a Web site, and face-to-face communications. However, one middle management staffer who joined CPM after the formation of PfC struggled during our interview to determine PfC's role. Even those who understand PfC do not necessarily love it. Weiner and Asselin note that in a city of 150,000, the six affiliates working together make a tough competitor for other human services organizations.

Cultural differences and resistance to change among some staff members appeared early in the process. However, trust in and communications between Weiner and Flores seem to have smoothed the process. Many of the staff we spoke with believed in Weiner's and Flores's genuine commitment to sharing information and discussing issues of concern to employees. The leaders, for example, made their expectations clear about how the creation of the MSO would require new competencies among staff. "You have to deal with people honestly," noted Flores. "Tell them if we don't do this, we're going to die, but, to continue to be with us, these are the skills you are going to need. . . . " Weiner described the importance of staff understanding, and feeling a stake in, the MSO. He told us, "It dawned on me one day that Flores and I were the only ones who saw the whole picture. So we began to work on this."

The trust in and among the leaders also seems to have allowed the organization to experiment without much backlash. In many of their efforts to establish and develop PfC, the leaders left a margin for error and for learning from mistakes. Flores noted that the written agreement between CPM and NEFWC to establish PfC has always been considered a "breathing document" allowing for considerable evolution in their relationship. The leaders of PfC have adopted a similar attitude in dealing with other affiliates, taking time to build trust and determine the most mutually beneficial relationship between the entities. The leaders have also told their staff that there will be mistakes, and that they hope staff will absorb the bumps in the road and learn from them. Weiner, for example, described how CPM, prior to the creation of the MSO, had flexible working hours, whereas NEFWC had more rigid rules about when employees worked. When the MSO leaders tried to implement CPM's policy with PfC staff, they found that the culture was not ready for it and had to backtrack.

Because PfC was created in part to reduce administrative costs, some management staff have had minor problems deciding when and how much to grow their administrative capacity as their programs grow. In other words, at what point does the ethic of reduction become too stringent? This exchange with Greim, chief operating officer of PfC, illustrates the challenge.

Greim: We're always trying to do more with less. When we get a new programmatic contract, it means that we'll have more administrative work to perform, as well. But this extra work doesn't necessarily create the need for an extra administrative position right away. So most of the time, we simply try to work a little harder. But it's obvious that at some points in time, the cumulative impact of having more programmatic contracts requires us to hire additional administrative staff so we can continue to provide quality management services. But our goal is to keep our marginal costs below our marginal administrative revenue.

Interviewer: So how do you determine . . . that you need to expand your administrative capacity?

Greim: In a perfect world, we'd have some sort of calculus for planning purposes. But for now, we basically know we need more staff when we see things starting to slow down, things not getting done timely or tasks falling through the cracks. Then we say, "What's going on? Maybe current staff is overextended and either we need to find more efficient ways to do the work or to we need to hire additional staff."

In addition to knowing when to grow, several of the people we spoke with were wondering *how* PfC would grow. Is an MSO just an evolutionary stage on the way to full-scale merger? Weiner reported that a few affiliates have discussed the possibility of merging with other affiliates as trust has grown and the benefits of affiliation have increased. Cruz, however, felt that the MSO may provide many of the benefits of a merger without giving up the identity of any organization.

Indeed, most of those we spoke with felt that the MSO will maintain its current structure and add more affiliates, perhaps one a year. Weiner and Flores's goal is to grow until the combined budgets of the affiliates equal about $100 million. Funders, banks, and prospective employees, in Flores's opinion, look at an organization of this size differently than at smaller institutions.

PfC has no timetable for reaching its $100 million goal. It plans to take advantage of opportunities as they arise, and gradually build associations that increase the MSO's capacity to serve its clients while decreasing the costs of doing so.

TRIART GALLERY AND GIFT SHOP

Overview of Partnership

Speed Art Museum, Kentucky Art and Craft Foundation, and Louisville Visual Art Association, the three major visual arts organizations in Louisville, Kentucky, created a limited liability company to jointly operate a gift store and gallery. (See Table A.5.)

Table A.5
Joint Venture Partnership

The Partners	Speed Art Museum	Kentucky Art and Craft Foundation (KACF)	Louisville Visual Art Association (LVAA)
Location	Louisville, Kentucky	Louisville, Kentucky	Louisville, Kentucky
Program Focus	Art/culture	Art/culture	Art/culture
Founded	1925	1981	1909
Approximate Annual Budget	$6.5 million	$1.4 million	$1.2 million
Number of Full-Time Equivalent Staff	60	16	18

Whom We Interviewed

John Begley
Executive Director
Louisville Visual Art Association

Brion Clinkingbeard
Curator/Director of Exhibitions
Kentucky Art and Craft Foundation, Inc.

Allan Cowen
President and CEO
Fund for the Arts

Holly French
Finance Director
Kentucky Art and Craft Foundation, Inc.

Robert W. Griffith
Board Member
J. B. Speed Art Museum

David C. Knopf
Business Manager
J. B. Speed Art Museum

Lou Lesher
Manager
TriArt Gallery

Mary Miller
Executive Director
Kentucky Art and Craft Foundation, Inc.

Peter Morrin
Director
J. B. Speed Art Museum

Anne Ogden
Administrative Director
J. B. Speed Art Museum

Marjorie Pitterman
Board Member
Louisville Visual Art Association

Rita Steinberg
Former Executive Director
Kentucky Art and Craft Foundation, Inc.

Patrick Welsh
Board Member
Kentucky Art and Craft Foundation, Inc.

Lisa Work
Associate Director
Louisville Visual Art Association

Anonymous

The Story of the Partnership

The idea had been percolating for a while. The Kentucky Art and Craft Foundation (KACF) and the Louisville Visual Art Association (LVAA) were both pinched for space, and their directors, Rita Steinberg and John Begley, respectively, had begun talking to each other about sharing space.

Around the same time, Speed Art Museum was preparing for a major renovation and looking for a way to be visible to the public while its facility was closed for construction. The museum's leaders also had some long-time public relations concerns on their minds. The mayor and others felt that moving the museum downtown would help with the economic development of the city. And when Speed received a major bequest in 1996, the pressure to move heightened. Speed decided, instead, to use these funds for acquisitions and for the endowment, but it was still looking for a way to have a downtown presence to address the concerns of its critics. Peter Morrin, Speed's director, wondered whether sharing space with other organizations would make the venture more economical.

Shortly after Morrin joined the conversations that Begley and Steinberg had begun, the stars seemed to align. The Fund for the Arts, a major supporter of arts organizations in Louisville, began offering incentive grants to encourage arts organizations to generate income. At around the same time, Morrin received a phone call from the manager of a new high-rise downtown, offering Speed free space on the first floor.

Steinberg, Morrin, and Begley quickly worked out a plan for a joint gallery and gift shop called TriArt. The parties had three primary goals: to demonstrate collaboration among the three organizations and thus show their solidarity and increase their visibility; to increase traffic at their respective organizations by using the downtown retail angle as a marketing tool; and to produce income from sales for the partner organizations. They did not assign priority to any of the goals.

Their next step was to go to their boards, not to discuss the idea but to present it and ask for approval. The boards, accustomed to following the lead of their directors, did approve it, but some members had reservations, particularly about the goals and whether these were important or even feasible. The Fund for the Arts's goal in providing funding was clear. It believed that traditional revenue streams for arts organizations were drying up and that these nonprofits would have to look for new ways to generate income. KACF and LVAA appeared to share this goal, but the staff and board of Speed were less interested in revenue generation. In fact, the Speed board was worried that if TriArt failed to produce income and become self sufficient, their organization, because of its resources, would be left holding the bag. However, Morrin, who had worked closely with the other directors, felt that Speed could trust them.

KACF and LVAA, both of which received ongoing support from the Fund for the Arts, were also interested in showing the Fund that they could cooperate. Allan Cowen, the president and CEO of the Fund, was an outspoken proponent of organizations working together to cut costs.

The three partners applied for support from the Fund for the Arts and received a $50,000 grant and a $50,000 no-interest loan. The project picked up speed at this point, both because the Fund grants were good for only one year and because the landlord wanted them in the space as soon as possible.

A steering committee, including the executive directors and one board member from each organization, began discussing the best way to formalize the partnership. The members considered a limited liability company (LLC), sharing space with separate retail operations, and forming a separate corporation in which the three organizations would be "shareholders." They chose an LLC because it allowed Speed to protect its considerable assets, facilitated the partners' pooling of resources, and gave the partners control over the business.

The partners hired several consultants with expertise in craft merchandising to review their plans for TriArt. The consultants felt that the venture was feasible but undercapitalized. So the three organizations started raising money. Their goal was to raise between $160,000 and $225,000. With the grant and loan from the Fund, as well as smaller contributions from other foundations and businesses, they raised just over the minimum goal. The steering committee also hired a manager for the TriArt gallery.

The plan was that each partner would produce two exhibits a year, using funds from the TriArt budget. The gallery opened during the Christmas season in 1996–97 and had good returns on the first show. However revenues were not high enough to cover expenses in the first year of the venture, even with an anticipated deficit built into the budget. Thus, each partner contributed cash at the end of the year. The required infusion made members of the three boards concerned, especially those who were skeptical at the outset.

In addition to failing to meet financial goals, the partnership was suffering from a weak management structure. Authority was too diffused. With three directors, all busy running their own organizations, the venture lacked strong leadership. So the steering committee decided to appoint a managing director to hold the whip. The committee chose Steinberg because she had the most retailing experience of the three directors.

Despite efforts to tighten control over the venture, the second year ended with a deficit. Although smaller than in the first year, the shortfall prompted another cash contribution from the partners. As the financial pressures heightened, some pushed to produce only shows that were likely to be lucrative. In addition, several retail consultants told the organizations that to make money, they should abandon the gallery and focus only on the gift shop. Thus began an ongoing debate about the mission of TriArt. Begley recalls that some involved felt that "we were corrupting our higher values" by choosing shows that were more likely to generate income.

Robert Griffith, of the Speed board, told us

the thing that made it possible for the museum to be involved in [TriArt] at all was the idea that we would do Speed Museum quality exhibitions. I was surprised at how quickly the financial pressure of making the gallery work got rid of that idea almost completely.

Some LVAA board members felt that it was not LVAA's mission to provide the community with a gift shop. Cowen, president of the Fund for the Arts, maintained throughout that an organization can generate revenues without compromising mission, and that lack of commitment to this idea (as well as lack of business acumen) was the downfall of the TriArt venture. However, Begley concluded, "Because the partner organizations had different missions, TriArt developed a mission that reflected each but did not match any of them directly."

While TriArt required the boards to contribute resources for a venture they were unsure of, it required staff members to contribute time to plan, install, market, and manage TriArt shows, all without extra pay. "This was something that I was very involved in," recalled Morrin,

but it did not have the same levels of ownership with other staff. It came at a time when I didn't think we could turn it down. It also came at a time when we were very busy getting ready for reinstallation of this facility and planning for major exhibitions. . . . So I think that was a flaw.

Some KACF staff members felt that they bore a disproportionate burden because their director at the time, Rita Steinberg, often took the lead in the partnership. Moreover, their bookkeeper was assigned the management of TriArt's finances.

Like a growing number of board members, there were staff members who did not think TriArt was good for their organization. Brion Clinkingbeard, the curator/director of exhibitions at KACF, felt that the time and other resources spent on a couple of the exhibitions that KACF produced at TriArt—which were among the most lucrative of the TriArt shows—would have been better spent on shows at KACF's main site. He believed his organization could have done a better job on the exhibitions in the larger space at KACF, and would not have had to split the proceeds.

TriArt faced another hurdle in overcoming negative press prompted by several for-profit gallery owners who believed that TriArt, subsidized by the Fund for the Arts and given a tax-exempt status, was unfairly competing with them. The TriArt leadership worked to explain to the gallery community that they would not duplicate artists that other galleries were showing. They also stressed that their primary audiences, convention center visitors and downtown workers, were underexposed markets. In addition, TriArt worked to bring attention to the Louisville gallery scene in general through a videotape and gallery guide. This strategy worked to some degree, but ultimately TriArt had trouble attracting business to itself, much less to others. And as TriArt faltered, the gallery owners quieted their complaints.

Logistical concerns also drained energy from the venture. Dealing with three boards (which together totaled 120 people) turned out to be more cumbersome than expected. The members of the steering committee did not feel that they could make significant decisions (such as approval of loans) without endorsement from their boards. Due to the schedules for the different board meetings, decisions would sometimes take months to make.

Marketing also became a challenge. The partner organizations originally planned to contribute the time and expertise of their respective marketing departments to promoting TriArt. But they found that these departments gave priority to their own institution's needs, and, according to Begley, "TriArt became the stepchild to each of the organizations."

In 1999, because of disappointing financial returns and because some felt that the financial information they were receiving from the KACF bookkeeper was incorrect, the partnering organizations formed a finance committee of board members from each partner. This committee met monthly along with board members of TriArt.

In the third year (which was supposed to be the break-even year) TriArt had a deficit of $6,000. The venture appeared, to a growing number of board and staff members, to be a drain on the human and financial resources of the partner organizations. Moreover, TriArt faced several crippling blows. Speed had reopened its main facility and was no longer interested in the visibility TriArt might have afforded it. Additionally, Steinberg, perhaps TriArt's biggest proponent, moved away, and Mary Miller, who took her place at KACF, had less interest in the project. The convention center, which was across the street from the gallery and provided much of the customer base, closed down for renovations, and Providian Insurance Company, one of the largest tenants in Aegon building, where TriArt was located, and a backer of the venture, moved to its Baltimore headquarters.

With these negative signs and without evidence thus far of the predicted benefits, discussion began in April 1999 about dissolving the partnership. Cowen suggested that KACF assume the space, and offered to forgive the Fund's $50,000 loan. Miller, her treasurer, and her board president explored this option, but her executive committee voted against it because the space was just four blocks from KACF's other retail operation, and the convention center traffic, even postconstruction, did not seem promising. LVAA considered the same deal. They decided that they could make it work if they discontinued the gallery and made it just a gift shop with items sold on consignment.

In January 2000, the TriArt oversight committee was disbanded. The gallery closed in March. With proceeds from a final sale, the participants were able to pay off a bank loan and most other invoices. The Fund forgave their loan, as promised. The gift shop reopened as "TryArt" in April 2000 under the sole auspices of LVAA.

Despite the turbulence of the partnership, Morrin and Begley are glad that they tried it, and most of those whom we interviewed agreed that the partnership had no lasting ill effects. "It was worth a try. It didn't pan out. . . . But it didn't kill us," concludes Begley.

We ended up with a better facility and site, and a more visible operation . . . [and] we are selling more regional art than we were prior to this and not having to subsidize the operation . . . so from our point of view, all of those things are positive.

The experience also seems to have given the participants a respect for the complexity of any business venture such as TriArt and for the added difficulties of joint management. For Miller the silver lining of the venture was that she got to know the leaders of the other organizations well, and now has a special bond with them—a bond that could lead to future joint efforts.

TALBERT HOUSE–CORE CASE

Overview of Partnership

Talbert House, a multipurpose human service organization in Cincinnati, Ohio, became the parent of Core Behavioral Health Care, a Cincinnati mental health agency. Through the partnership, the organizations have consolidated their administrative functions, their policies and procedures, and some of their programs. Core pays Talbert a management fee for the administrative services. Talbert's board appoints Core's board, and three Core members sit on Talbert's board. Core's executive director reports to Talbert's director, but the Core board retains significant input to hire and fire its leader. (See Table A.6.)

Whom We Interviewed

Paul A. Guggenheim
Executive Director
Core Behavioral Health Centers

Tom Kilcoyne
Board Member
Talbert House, Inc.

Table A.6
Parent-Subsidiary Partnership

The Partners	Talbert House	Core Behavioral Health Care
Location	Cincinnati, Ohio	Cincinnati, Ohio
Program Focus	Human services, multipurpose	Mental health
Founded	1965	1973
Approximate Annual Budget	$29 million	$5.6 million
Number of Full-Time Equivalent Staff	520	95

Robert T. Lameier
Board Member
Core Behavioral Health Centers

Pam McClain
Vice President
Talbert House, Inc.

Katie McGuire
Public Relations and Communications
Talbert House, Inc.

Clyde Miller
Manager, 281-CARE
Talbert House, Inc.

Michael P. Oberdoerster
Medical Director
Core Behavioral Health Centers

Russell Peguero-Winters
Director of Case Management
Core Behavioral Health Centers

Stuart Schloss
Board Member
Core Behavioral Health Centers

Roger Smith
Clinical Director
Core Behavioral Health Centers

Neil Tilow
President and CEO
Talbert House, Inc.

Patrick Tribbe
President/CEO
Hamilton County Community Mental Health Board

The Story of the Partnership

When the public agencies on which Talbert House and Core Behavioral Health Centers depended for funds started sending new signals, Talbert and Core paid attention. The organizations' leaders and board members had heard that some of their largest funders—such as the Hamilton County Community Mental Health Board—were looking for ways to reduce costs by managing fewer contracts. Both organizations came to the same conclusion: they needed to be of a certain size to persist, and only by growing could they continue to win contracts and keep their costs down.

Patrick Tribbe, of the Mental Health Board, reflected Talbert and Core's concerns. "We had a review process for our levy. Our levy comes up roughly every five years. One of the recommendations from that group was to try to have fewer contract agencies," he recounted.

We have 45 providers but 8 or 9 of those make up the bulk of our contract money . . . So what you have is a multitude of contracts that are in the 150,000–$200,000 range by some very specialty niche providers . . . The difficulty is it costs us just as much to manage a contract that is $150,000 as it does with a $10 million agency [which receives larger contracts], and they sometimes need more technical assistance. You're talking about agencies that don't have a financial officer, HR folk, but they need those services, and they have to purchase it. . . .

Tribbe also said that his agency pushes grantees "very hard" to combine and work together as closely as possible.

Paul Guggenheim, Core's executive director, said that a national consultant specializing in behavioral health agencies also influenced his thinking. When asked what it would take, in the future, for a behavioral health care agency to make it, the consultant said that such an organization would need at least $20 million in revenues to achieve sufficient economies of scale. She also said that the funds did not need to come from one agency, but could be spread over partner organizations.

The board and managers of Core did not see a way to grow on their own. They did not foresee the availability of much new funding for mental health services for adults. Indeed, the dollars seemed to be increasingly flowing toward children's programs. They also thought that Core was too small to have influence with funders. As Robert Lameier, a Core board member, graphically put it, "We're almost like dogs on leashes. I mean when the funding source jerks us one direction, we in a sense have to respond to that. . . . I would like to think that over a period of time we could develop much stronger input to the person that's yanking the leash."

So Core staff and board members started to think about consolidation. But they also looked at another avenue to increase their revenues. They thought about creating a public and a private arm under the umbrella of the agency. According to Dr. Michael Oberdoerster, then medical director for Core and now medical director for both organizations:

the dilemma that we had was we treat severely mentally disabled people, which is our primary mission, but staff felt that private pay clients might be scared off when they saw these clients in the waiting room. So there were pieces of our business that we thought were our primary mission which in some ways conflicted with trying to set up a private arm unless we duplicated costs by having a separate building . . . and that would make us less competitive because then you have a separate secretary, a separate medical records system . . . it would move us away from being the most competitive. Instead of consolidating our costs, it would be expanding our costs.

In addition to the problems inherent in the privatization idea, there was another strong force pushing the board to consolidate. Core predicted that a round of mergers would occur in human services, and they wanted to be ahead of the pack, to have more say in their future. Stuart Schloss, a Core board member, explained the thinking: if Core was at the front end, they felt, its leaders could help "write the structure" and ensure that it was well treated. An agency that decided to remain independent while others consolidated might find its funding in jeopardy as contracts went to the larger organizations. If such an agency decided to consolidate too late, there might be fewer potential partners available, and those might be bigger, giving the organization less leverage.

So the Core board and leaders began thinking about what type of partner might be best for them. They were interested in one that complimented their services and geographic focus rather than duplicating what they did. The also wanted a partner with strong community and governmental connections and a similar interest in growth.

For Talbert House, concerns about size and revenues arose as part of a larger strategic planning effort in 1995. Already a large organization offering a range of services, Talbert did not feel so threatened as Core. However, they did feel that to thrive in the future they would need to grow even more, and that the most efficient way would be through partnerships. Talbert's goals were similar to Core's. It wanted to find a partner that offered different services from Talbert's, particularly with regard to mental health, an area where it had some programs but lacked strong expertise. Core was on the top of Talbert's list for this reason, and because it would help Talbert to expand into new areas of Cincinnati.

In the fall of 1996, Neil Tilow, president of Talbert, set up a lunch date with Guggenheim, whom he had come to know through other behavioral health care collaborations, to discuss sharing a building on the west side of town. Although the deal fell through, the lunch was the first of several conversations about the potential benefits of working together as a way to cut costs and improve services. By January 1997 the two were ready to discuss the possibility of a partnership with representatives of their boards. After signing an agreement to explore a partnership, a joint committee of management staff and two board members from each organization was formed, and its meetings kept somewhat confidential.

The group considered the costs and benefits of both a subsidiary relationship and a full merger. "The full merger had lots of advantages in terms of being efficient, quick, done with, you move on, but it also had disadvantages," recalls Tilow. "You had the brand name. You had the staff who were interested in remaining part of Core, and you had a committed board. " Tilow also noted the disadvantages of size. "Contract sources say, 'I don't want to do this with Talbert House. They get all of the contracts. We don't need a monopoly. We need as many options as we can get.' . . . By maintaining brand names, we hoped to ease the fear that we were becoming the dominant player in town."

The Core board was divided on the idea of affiliation. The members who approached it more positively tended to be people who had been involved with similar partnerships and mergers in the business world. Some, according to Guggenheim, were "beneficially paranoid" about being taken over, and wondered who would be in control. They also wanted to know how they might get out of a relationship that wasn't working. Board members who were related to consumers of Core's services were very concerned that services remain the same and that clients not be affected. Although no one said that they were leaving because of the affiliation, some individuals left the board once the decision was made.

Attorneys on the two boards proposed, and the boards approved, a parent-subsidiary relationship. This type of relationship is rather complex, at least in comparison to other forms of strategic restructuring partnerships. Both organizations restructured their bylaws so that Core became a membership organization with Talbert as its only member. As its member, Talbert would have the authority to appoint Core's board. At the time the parent-subsidiary was formed in 1998, Talbert reappointed all existing Core board members. Three Core members—the past, current, and future Core board chairs—sit on Talbert's board as well as on Talbert's personnel and finance committees. Guggenheim became a staff member of Talbert at the level of vice president and reported to Tilow, but the Core board retained significant input to hire and fire its leader. In addition, his role as "executive director" of Core was maintained in order to identify the separate corporation as a subsidiary and to avoid confusing employees of Talbert House by the "vice president" designation.

Determining the structure and governance arrangements was relatively easy. The hard part was hammering out a management agreement that would specify who would do what and how they would be compensated. After much discussion, it was determined that five of Core's executive managers, in addition to its executive director, would work for Talbert and be contracted in part or in full back to Core. At the time of our interviews, the contract amounted to 10 percent of Core's budget, although the amount and percentages of staff time are negotiated on an annual basis. A key aspect of the agreement was its duration. There was established what Schloss describes as "a five-year honeymoon to quell fears." The idea was to assure those with both organizations that there was a trial period, but it was a fairly long trial period because the negotiators did not want either partner to drop out before they had a chance to make it work.

Although the management agreement spelled out the broad structure, there were, and continue to be, many details to work out. For example, the Core board did not want to cede control over their personnel policy to Talbert. After much negotiation, Tilow says he put his foot down: "I didn't think it could succeed if people were working side by side with different vacations, tuition reimbursement, etc. Such things represent the basic culture of an organization."

Tilow and Guggenheim met with both boards and staffs to explain the nature and limits of the partnership. When Tilow went to the county commissioners and representatives of Talbert and Core's major payer sources to tell them about the impending affiliation, he says that they almost applauded. Many, according to Tilow, felt that they were paying too many nonprofits too much for overhead expenses, and brightened at the prospect of a partnership that might help the organizations to economize.

A series of memos explaining the affiliation and a couple of meetings with all of the employees of each organization followed an initial announcement to staff. Tilow and Guggenheim promised no layoffs and made it clear that the goal was not to reduce expenditures, but instead to increase the buying power of both agencies.

After the affiliation became official in January 1998, the managers saw that to make the finances of the partnership work, the organizations needed to integrate their financial systems under one person. Thus, when Talbert's financial director left, Core's financial director moved to Talbert to work for both organizations. She had some trouble adjusting to the job, and left in 2000. This difficult transition was made even more so because the prior director had not tracked the costs of certain functions performed by one organization for the other. So the new director was significantly handicapped in developing realistic budgets. At the time of our interviews, some people felt that unfair costs were being imposed on one organization or the other, and management was working to address inequities.

Integrating mental health programming was also a thorny job. The leadership of the organizations felt that they could offer adult mental health and case management services more efficiently and effectively together by sharing expertise and consolidating management. So they decided to integrate Talbert's Substance Abuse/Mental Illness (SA/MI) services with Core's Partial Hospitalization, Case Management, and Respite Care programs. A small group of case management supervisors from both organizations met every other week to integrate policies and procedures and to consolidate supervision. These meetings were very contentious at first. Some SA/MI staff members felt they were being dismantled, and it was difficult for those on both sides not to be defensive about their programs. The consolidation of the programs resulted in the appointment of the Core clinical director (now a Talbert House employee) to oversee the integrated program. Some staff moved to new locations with new supervisors and, in some cases, staff from one organization was supervised by staff from the other.

Early on, the two organizations also looked at where all of their clients lived, and found that their services overlapped in only one part of the city. In this neighborhood, they created a "one-stop shop" where services of both organizations could be located in the same building, making access to programs easier for clients and reducing overhead expenses. "We are also marketing a couple of our programs together, but mainly the partnership is invisible to our clients," said Guggenheim. "While we always include in our materials that we are an affiliate of Talbert House, we want to keep Core a separate marketable entity."

Managed care turned out to not be so imminent in Cincinnati as the leadership of both organizations predicted in the mid-1990s. However, some staff members believe that their outcome-driven philosophy, tightened purse strings, and improved management information systems will make them ready to compete in a managed care environment that demands more accountability.

In the meantime, those involved generally acknowledge several advantages of the affiliation. Perhaps the most noticeable one, from the point of view of staff, is that benefits have improved as a result of the organizations' increased buying power. Additionally, some staff reported that working for a larger entity makes them feel that their job is more secure and that there is more room for promotion within the organization.

Pooling the resources of the two organizations has also allowed the partnership to hire higher quality management staff who have the experience and expertise to manage the now more complex organizations. And each organization has benefited from the knowledge and skills of the other organization's staff. Several people we spoke with as part of the case study particularly stressed the knowledge that Core senior staff brought to Talbert, including expertise in medical records, medical services, and mental health. A cross section of staff have learned about the capabilities of their partner organization's employees through participating in various joint committees charged with developing uniform policies and procedures in different functional areas. The process of making these decisions through consensus has been very time-consuming, but has allowed staff to get to know and learn from each other.

Perhaps most important, the organizations have been able to document savings. Findings from a study of the organizations' financial records by the University of Cincinnati confirmed that, if Talbert House were to provide the services that it provided in 1999 at 1997 per-unit costs, the overall cost to the organization would have been far greater. However, the study also indicated that, while Core had demonstrated at least some cost cutting within most of its service areas, there was an overall increase in the cost of operations since cost increases in one particular category of service minimized overall cost savings.

The University of Cincinnati study also found that both organizations were shifting resources, providing new services, and altering existing services, and that the shift in resources has allowed the agencies to increase the total number of services provided. Several interviewees felt that the partnership allowed the organizations more flexibility in treating dually diagnosed clients—those with both mental health problems (Core's area of expertise) and chemical dependency issues (an expertise of Talbert's).

Many aspects of the partnership have taken longer to develop and implement than expected. Interviewees described how efforts to include representatives from both organizations in decisions have led to a significant increase in the amount of time spent in meetings. Indeed, the joint committees that developed the new policies and procedures took twice as long as expected. The time spent in such meetings is what one Talbert staff member called a "hidden cost" of strategic restructuring.

Those we spoke with also described significant differences in how Talbert House and Core made decisions prior to the affiliation, and in the professional philosophies of staff members. Such differences caused cultural clashes. Several persons described Talbert as more bureaucratic but also more concerned about making decisions on a consensus basis than Core, where unilateral decisions were made. Contrasting professional backgrounds caused conflicts as well, particularly when the parties decided to consolidate the mental health services of both agencies under the supervision of a Core manager. Many Talbert direct-service staff came from a chemical dependency orientation that focused on short-term therapies and on helping clients to take responsibility for their actions. By contrast, Core provided more long-term services to mentally disabled adults and took a more nurturing approach. Additionally, some Core staff felt that Core had more of a culture of professionalism and accountability than Talbert. The intensity of cultural clashes has waned over time as staff members have adjusted and new staff members, without fidelity to either way of life, have come on board.

Another challenge of the partnership has been making it clear to everyone involved just what the partnership *is*. The complexity of the relationship between Talbert and Core has led to persistent confusion among some staff about the identities of their organizations. The partial mixing of staff and policies is particularly confusing in the mental health area, where Talbert employees are reporting to Core supervisors. Moreover, just what it means to be a parent and a subsidiary is not always apparent. For example, Tilow described Core as both under Talbert's control but also as a customer of its administrative services. "In that respect, it's not parent to subsidiary, its more peer to peer," explained Tilow. "And when you can do that, it's a lot healthier relationship because people will work harder if they can really drive more of the decisions and make a bigger impact."

The confusion around identity may have been caused or exacerbated by a lack of effective communication to staff members. The University of Cincinnati study findings state,

Our review of the two previously conducted employee surveys shows that, although Talbert House and Core are committed to their employees, both organizations have failed in some way to communicate their vision for the affiliation. We believe that senior management may need to address and remedy employee concerns. (Zandvakili & Rafales, 2000)

Similarly, a report on the results of a 2000 survey of Core employees notes, "While most understood the need for affiliation with Talbert House, less than half feel that they have been kept current in connection with the Talbert House affiliation" (Training, 2000).

Another topic of debate among those involved concerns the right ratio of joint decision making to unilateral leadership. Some staff members felt that the decision to involve a wide range of people in planning the integration of the mental health services and in the policy and procedures groups allowed staff to get to know one another and to make informed decisions. However, others felt that while involving staff in planning was a good idea, the leadership should have made some important decisions up front. One staff member said, for example, that cultural differences should have been examined and made explicit to staff at the beginning, and that the leadership should have made a determination about how much difference was acceptable. Another staff member thought it unfair to involve staff in integration decisions that might ultimately cost them their jobs.

Although some of the leaders' decisions were unpopular, their personalities appear to have been critical to the process of integration. Tilow stressed that the senior staff bought into the affiliation and did not sabotage it. Board and staff members noted that Guggenheim was able to "put his ego aside" and make decisions that were best for Core rather than for himself. Others noted that the stability of the leadership at both organizations allowed them to weather the challenges of an intensive restructuring. Perhaps the most important decision of the leadership was to acknowledge that the implementation process would inevitably involve making mistakes and that the process would take time. By setting these expectations, they seem to have prevented some discouragement among staff.

Still, some people we spoke with felt that, despite its advantages, the partnership is not sustainable in the long term. The multiple payrolls and allocation issues are a nightmare, according to medical director Michael Oberdoerster. To him, such complexities argue for a full-scale merger at some point in the future. Pam McClain, a vice president at Talbert House, also thought a merger was probably in the future and noted that a logical time might be when Guggenheim retired.[2]

Tilow, on the other hand, thought that, although a merger was possible, he had yet to be convinced it was the best outcome for the agencies. He stressed the downsides of a merger: the loss of the Core brand name and the risk of igniting concerns among funders and others that Talbert would be a monopoly.

If not toward a merger, then where is the affiliation heading? Most involved agreed that the organizations are now so intertwined that it would be quite difficult to go back to operating independently. However, Guggenheim felt that, if Core's identity were threatened or if it lost significant funds as a result of the affiliation, it might consider pulling out.

Some of the people we interviewed wondered if there was a better way to structure the relationship. Tom Kilcoyne, of the Talbert board, worried that the two organizations were still budgeting separately, and that it was not clear what would happen if one of the subsidiaries began to have budgetary problems.[3] Although, technically, Talbert did not have an obligation to bail Core out, Kilcoyne said the reality was that Talbert would not want the subsidiaries to default because that would reflect badly on Talbert. He thought that a more logical structure would be that of a corporate parent, which would control and provide consolidated administrative services to several subsidiaries, one for each program area. This would be a clearer relationship than now exists between the two organizations. The subsidiaries would not have their own boards, and program areas of the subsidiaries would not overlap. Another structure that might work, in his opinion, would be to have several nonprofit operating corporations that would own and receive services from a for-profit management service organization.

Perhaps the most likely scenario, at least for the short term, is that the two organizations will continue to hone their relationship, integrating more of their operations. And Talbert may consider adding more subsidiaries (in addition to the partnerships with Core and the Center for Children and Families) to increase its scale and the range of services offered to clients. The partnership is still very much in formation, and it may be years before the partners reach any sort of homeostasis.

ACHIEVE

Overview of Partnership

Zonta Services and Peninsula Children's Center, two agencies that provided educational, mental health, and other services to children with physical and mental disabilities in the San Francisco Bay Area, dissolved their organizations and merged all of their administrative and programmatic functions to become a new agency called ACHIEVE. (See Table A.7.)

Whom We Interviewed

Larry Brenner
Former Staff Member
ACHIEVE

Table A.7
Merger

The Original Organizations	Zonta Services	Peninsula Children's Center
Location	San Jose, California	Palo Alto, California
Program Focus	Education and other services for severely impaired children and those with developmental disabilities and mental illness	Education and other services for severely impaired children and those with developmental disabilities and mental illness
Founded	1962	1960
Approximate Annual Budget	$1.7 million	$3 million
Number of Full-Time Equivalent Staff	46	60

Deirdre Cochran
Former Executive Director
Zonta Services

Tom Dreschler
School Director
ACHIEVE

Patricia Gardner
Former Staff Member
ACHIEVE

Jeannette Glasser
Clinical Director
ACHIEVE

Kathy Kalm
Teacher
ACHIEVE

Leland Levy
Board Member
ACHIEVE

Jim Patterson
Former Board Member
ACHIEVE

Philip Pinsukanjana
Former Staff Member
ACHIEVE

Carol Pliner
Board Member
ACHIEVE

Magaly Ramos-Cartagena
School Director
ACHIEVE

Jean Spurr
Director of Human Resources
ACHIEVE

Gail Switzer
Executive Director
ACHIEVE

Story of the Partnership

They weren't large enough. This was the impression that Deirdre Cochran, director of Zonta Services in the late 1990s, was getting. Zonta, a school for children with disabilities that made it difficult for them to attend regular schools, never had more than fifty kids on campus. Foundation officers often asked how their services differed from other, larger organizations with similar students. And more and more often she was hearing talk about managed care. The local county mental health boards, on which Zonta and similar agencies like Peninsula Children's Center (PCC) depended for a large portion of their funds, put the word out that they wanted organizations to cooperate, said a long-time board member at Zonta; "It was implied. It wasn't specific pressure where they came to us and said, 'Look, if you guys don't merge we are not going to fund you.'" The story was that the mental health boards were strapped and felt they could reduce their expenses by contracting with fewer agencies, and that those agencies could be more efficient if they took advantage of economies of scale by combining. Adding to the pressure was the fact that two large mental health organizations in the area had already merged. Cochran, and Gail Switzer, then director of PCC, were concerned that their organizations would lose vital contracts unless they grew.

Five years later, when we interviewed staff and board members of the two agencies, which eventually merged to form ACHIEVE, it was not clear whether the story was taking longer than expected to reach its natural conclusion or whether the predictions had been wrong. Managed care—and its various efficiency measures—had not (at least yet) taken hold in the area, leaving some who had lived through the merger wondering whether what a former Zonta board member called the "pain and turmoil" of the consolidation had been necessary.

Both Zonta and PCC had considered various consolidations for a number of years before they went through with the merger that resulted in ACHIEVE. The Association Of Mental Health Contract Agencies in Santa Clara County—of which both PCC and Zonta were members—had spent two or three years looking at developing an umbrella corporation that would contract on behalf of the member agencies. The association hired a consultant who examined and recommended the strategy, but shortly thereafter some of the larger agencies backed out, leaving the smaller agencies feeling even more vulnerable. The smaller groups got together and talked about collaborative structures, according to Switzer, but those discussions never really went anywhere. Nor did conversations that PCC had with a few other agencies about a joint management information system. "It always fell short," recalled Switzer, "because each agency's individual interest and concerns and timing never matched the others."

Although these attempts at partnering failed, the belief that partnering would be essential to survival remained strong among staff members at PCC and particularly at Zonta, the smaller of the two agencies. "I'm not aware that another strategy [besides merger] was considered," noted Magaly Ramos-Cartagena, who worked for Zonta before the merger. "The other option was not to merge, not to survive, knowing that we might not survive, and [that] to disappear as an agency . . . was the other option."

Switzer and Cochran began to talk about a possible merger. The organizations had considered a merger several years earlier as a result of the similarity of their missions and philosophies, but the fact that PCC was unionized made the cost of merging (i.e., of raising Zonta staff salaries and benefits) prohibitive. However, by the mid-1990s, the threat of managed care seemed strong enough to warrant a second look.

The two boards agreed to form a joint committee to conduct a feasibility study on a possible merger. The study involved interviewing staff members, board members, funders, and other stakeholders. During this time, the organizations discovered that, not only did they both provide educational, mental health, and other services to children with physical and mental disabilities, they also seemed to compliment each other administratively. PCC had a stronger development department than Zonta, which had just hired its first development director, and a fairly well-established private fundraising base. Zonta offered an experienced finance director, which PCC needed because Switzer had been doing all the financial work for her agency—a task that was becoming burdensome. Although some individuals we spoke with felt that the merger would not and did not benefit their programs, others, like Jean Spurr, who worked with PCC before the merger, felt that Zonta had a strong vocational training program, which PCC lacked, and PCC had a mental health program more integrated into the entire program than Zonta's was.

Based on the feasibility study and the growing concerns among staff about future funding, in September 1995 the joint committee recommended, and the boards passed, a resolution approving a "fifty-fifty merger." Those on both sides felt that Zonta would not agree to an unequal consolidation. However it was not clear what "fifty-fifty" meant specifically, beyond the boards' decision to retain both executive directors as co-directors of the new organization. Because of the delay in attaining 501(c)(3) status for the new agency, the organizations operated legally as separate entities until July 1996.

The implementation plan seemed as logical as the merger itself. Together, the directors encouraged staff at all levels to meet with their counterparts from what was the other organization and report on similarities and differences in the programs. The organizations hired a popular former Zonta executive director as program services director to help integrate the programs. They also hired a consultant to help develop a shared vision. The former executive director, financial director, and development director at Zonta moved into offices at the Palo Alto site.

Unfortunately, it did not take long for the logical process to begin to unravel. It became apparent to most of the management staff early on that the shared directorship was not working. Although Switzer was to oversee administrative functions and Cochran programmatic ones, staff reported that they often did not know who had the authority on many issues. Similarly, funders wanted to know who had ultimate responsibility for the organization.

Leadership styles and staff cultures were also clashing. The members of PCC's management team had been around a long time, and Switzer's management was largely laissez faire. Cochran, who was younger than Switzer, had less administrative experience and a more hands-on style of leadership. After the merger, Cochran relocated to the Palo Alto (formerly PCC) site, and Zonta staff, left with only one administrator at their site, felt abandoned and confused as to where to find direction and authority. PCC staff, unaccustomed to close direction, was skeptical about reporting to the Zonta director. The two directors were careful not to step on each other's toes, but as a result provided no clear leadership to the organization.

In the fall of 1996, Cochran asked the board to make a decision between the two directors. Over the next seven to eight months, the board interviewed staff members and representatives of other organizations that dealt with ACHIEVE. During this time, loyalties solidified among staff and board members and fears mounted about how the choice of one or the other director would affect individual positions and the organization as a whole. Moreover, the process of integrating programs and operations halted.

The board finally decided that Switzer's longer experience with administration made her the better candidate. This decision exacerbated feelings among formerly Zonta staff that, despite the rhetoric about the fifty-fifty merger, PCC had taken over Zonta.

The staffs from both sides were also having trouble adjusting to a larger organization in which once family-like atmospheres transformed into a more formal, hierarchical structure. This was particularly striking for formerly Zonta staff, who had not been unionized and found the contentiousness of union negotiations quite different from the way they had interacted with management before the merger. Moreover, Switzer was not able to sustain her plans to spend two days a week at the San Jose site, accentuating feelings of abandonment among the formerly Zonta staff.

Without strong direction, staff began pulling in different directions. Some were distrustful of others' motives, and some dug in their heels, resisting attempts to integrate the two sites. In some people's view, this contentious atmosphere made the leadership reluctant to appoint managers from one organization or the other.

Thus they maintained co-managers, such as the school directors and mental health directors, with no clear plan about what to do with the extra staff. Additionally the distance between the sites (approximately 20 miles, a long distance given traffic in the area) remained an immutable variable, confounding attempts at integration.

When asked to describe the differences between the two former organizations, staff and board members from both sides provided relatively consistent views—although with negative or positive slants depending on their perspectives. PCC staff alternatively was seen as complainers or as not afraid to express their opinions to management. They were also described as "laid-back" and diverse in their viewpoints. Zonta employees, by contrast, were described as compliant to authority, detail-oriented, and united around a single philosophy. Those on both sides recounted their initial surprise at the differences in cultures. "You don't realize you have a culture until something like this happens," noted Switzer.

The importance and persistence of organizational culture emerged in many interviews with staff and board members. Patricia Gardner, former development director for PCC and then ACHIEVE, pointed out that many people choose to work at a nonprofit because of the mission as well as the culture of the organization, which arises from its policies, procedures, vocabulary, attitudes toward clients, and even dress code. The deep roots of organizational culture are clear when one considers that some formerly Zonta staff referred to the room numbers that corresponded to certain classes in their former facility long after they moved into a new building with different room numbers.

To help bring the two sites, which in some ways continued to operate like separate organizations, together, ACHIEVE hired a consultant to develop an integration plan. However, the leadership seemed to lack resolution and energy in implementing it. Many staff and board members have spoken, both directly and indirectly, about a need for a clear idea about the amount and quality of integration possible and necessary in a merger of organizations that remained physically separate. Switzer's attempts to spend time at the San Jose site, attempts to bring the staff together at midway locations for meetings and parties, and other integration efforts have diminished over the years. Although inertial forces are occasionally overcome by an individual staff member who sees benefit in sharing expertise and joint planning between sites, and although administrative functions have been consolidated at the Palo Alto site, the sites function without much interaction or common vision.

The only positive effect of the merger that the majority of interviewees agreed on was that clients have benefited from a wider range of services. The San Jose site (formerly Zonta) now has after-school and early childhood programs, and the Palo Alto site (formerly PCC) now has a preschool program. In addition, having two sites has provided families with a choice of locations. Unionization was a benefit to Zonta workers, according to almost half of those we spoke to, and a few felt strongly that the survival of Zonta's program was an important outcome of the consolidation.

Two of the board members interviewed remained unconvinced that a merger was necessary or the best strategy. They suggested that board members considering recommendations for consolidation from their directors do independent research to feel confident that the potential benefits outweigh the significant costs (financial and otherwise) of merging. Most of those we spoke with recommended dealing with difficult issues—such as selection of the management staff and how the programs would or would not be integrated—up front, and then developing a budget and monitoring strategy to support the plan.

At the time of our interviews, a changing of the guard was occurring at ACHIEVE. Switzer and several other administrators had left or were about to leave. Budget cuts had resulted in a reduction of programs at ACHIEVE. Echoing the sentiment of many interviewees, an ACHIEVE staff member said, "It's sad to see some leave after 30 years of tenure, but it's also an exciting opportunity to really breathe new life into the place. And [the new leadership will be] a completely neutral third party not aligned with anything. Because I think everyone is clear that it has to be somebody from the outside." Some staff members hoped that a new director would be able to bring about some of the changes that were originally supposed to occur with the merger, such as streamlining operations and integrating programs. However, others saw the two sites drifting farther apart and operating more independently with time.

NOTES

1. Interviewed in 1999 as part of the Phase I study.

2. Several months after our interviews, Guggenheim took a job elsewhere and a new director for Core was hired.

3. A year and a half after the Talbert–Core partnership began, Mental Health Services East (later renamed Center for Children and Families) also became a subsidiary of Talbert House.

APPENDIX B

Methodology (Overview)

This book is primarily based on the findings of Phase II of the two-part national study on strategic restructuring. Phase I was conducted to identify the primary types of strategic restructuring partnerships that had been implemented by non-profits in the United States. The goal of Phase II was to look more deeply into the experiences of several organizations in various types of partnerships and to improve understanding of the prevalence of strategic restructuring as well as its potential impact on the nonprofit sector in the future.

PHASE I

The research team administered a structured survey by telephone or through an on-line survey instrument to a convenience sample of respondents whose organizations had experience with strategic restructuring. Organizations were limited to social services and cultural organizations in the nonprofit sector in the United States that had been, were currently, or planned to be involved in the sharing or merging of boards, space, equipment, facilities, personnel, risk, and/ or administrative systems with other organizations.[1] Respondents were recruited in a number of ways. The research team publicized the survey through announcements in publications, newsletters, Web sites, and E-mail mailing lists focused on nonprofit issues, and requested referrals from organizations that consult with, fund, and manage associations of nonprofits. We also asked for referrals from respondents to the survey. Respondents (N = 192) were individuals—primarily directors—who represented one of the organizations involved in a strategic re-structuring. Each completed a brief questionnaire.

The research team reviewed respondents' descriptions of their partnerships and identified two primary factors that distinguished strategic restructurings: level of integration and area of integration (programmatic, administrative, or both). We devised a typology that included two primary types and six subtypes of restructuring. (See Partnership Matrix.) Several other researchers reviewed the categories and the definitions of each. We then assigned strategic restructurings from the sample to the categories. We tested the taxonomy by having a researcher who was not involved in the project assign a subsample of partnerships to categories, and by comparing her assignments to those of the research team.

PHASE II

Case Studies

We conducted six case studies focusing on partnerships that have been in existence for at least one year and are representative of the categories identified in Phase I. We chose case study sites from the Phase I sample, aiming to include a range of types of organizations in terms of size, program focus, and location. Partnerships involving no more than three primary partner organizations were selected because we had limited time to make site visits and conduct interviews. Data was collected through semistructured interviews with multiple stakeholders (such as directors, board members, staff, and funders) at each organization involved in each selected partnership. We conducted 9 to 15 interviews for each case and 65 interviews in total. (See first list of interviewees in Appendix E.) We chose subjects with the assistance of the executive directors of the participating organizations, who were asked to identify a group of subjects that represented a variety of perspectives on the partnership. In all cases, we interviewed the executive director and a middle or senior level manager at the primary partner organizations. We also collected some written documentation from each site, including meeting minutes, publicity materials, published articles, and legal documents. Interviews primarily focused on the motivations, benefits, costs, challenges, and lessons of the partnership experience from each interviewee's point of view. Interview summaries were developed and sent to each subject for review and editing. The corrected versions of the interviews were coded and analyzed for dominant themes.

Prevalence Survey

To gain a larger sense of the prevalence of partnerships among nonprofits, we conducted a telephone survey of 400 nonprofits that provided human services or arts and culture programs or services and had total revenues greater than or equal to $200,000 in two cities, San Francisco and Cleveland. In each city, we telephoned a random sample of nonprofits to determine whether they had formed partnerships, and if so, when. We followed up by E-mail, fax, and U.S. mail with those organizations that could not be reached by phone. Two hundred sixty-two organizations responded to the survey. We also collected some information on motivations, benefits, and costs from 36 organizations that volunteered to discuss their strategic restructuring experience. (For a more detailed review of the survey methodology, see Appendix C.)

Interviews with National Nonprofit Leaders

We shared preliminary, partial findings from the case studies and prevalence survey with 20 national nonprofit leaders, including leaders of national nonprofits, national foundations, and national nonprofit associations. (See second list of interviewees in Appendix E.) We conducted individual telephone interviews with them about their reflections on the findings, and about their views of the current and future effects of strategic restructuring partnerships on the nonprofit sector as a whole, and on the social service sector in particular.

NOTE

1. For the purposes of the study, we defined *social service and cultural organizations* as organizations providing direct service, advocacy, or volunteer support on one or more of the following issues/concerns, or as a membership organization for other organizations providing such services, advocacy, or volunteer support: public protection; employment/jobs; food, nutrition, agriculture; housing/shelter; public safety; disaster preparedness and relief; recreation, leisure, sports, athletics; youth development; human services: multipurpose and other; arts, culture, and humanities; mental health, crisis intervention; religion-related/spiritual development. To be an eligible respondent, an organization had to fit this definition, but its partner organization(s) could fall outside the definition.

Methodology and Findings from Prevalence Survey

METHODOLOGY

Sample selection was based on data from financial forms filed with the Internal Revenue Service (called 990 forms) by nonprofits that have more than $25,000 annual revenue and are incorporated under section 501(c)(3) of the Internal Revenue Code.

In order to determine the prevalence of strategic restructuring among nonprofits, we drew a random sample of 400 nonprofit organizations from a pool of 840 organizations with the following characteristics.

- Annual revenues of $200,000 or more based on financial data primarily from fiscal year 1998.
- Organizations that indicated on their 990 forms that they primarily provide human services[1] or services related to the arts, culture, or humanities.
- Organizations located in San Francisco, California (N = 262), and Cleveland, Ohio (N = 138). We chose these cities due to the interests of the funders of the study and based on the assumption that, if we chose two urban areas that had fairly high concentrations of nonprofits, we were more likely to find strategic restructuring activity. The size of the randomly selected sample chosen from each city is based on roughly half of the population of nonprofits in each city that fit the specifications.

The primary mode of contact with sampled organizations was by telephone. We made at least three follow-up phone calls to each organization that did not respond to the initial call and, in a large number of cases, sent E-mails and faxes as well. All nonrespondents to phone calls, E-mails, or faxes (who had not declined to participate) also received survey forms via the U.S. mail. We collected information from 256 organizations, which represented 70 percent of our corrected sample size of 367 (the number of organizations for which we found contact information and no indication that they had closed or moved out of the target city).

To determine if respondents had strategic restructuring partnership experience, we asked several structured questions regarding the key aspects of our definition of strategic restructuring including whether the respondents had ever been in an organizational partnership that involved the sharing, transferring, or consolidation of services, resources, or programs; and whether any such partnerships involved a continuing commitment for the foreseeable future, shared or transferred decision-making authority over programmatic or administrative functions, and a formal agreement among the organizations. We also asked a question to rule out partnerships limited to sharing information, coordinating programs, or conducting joint planning (see survey form, Appendix D).

We attempted to collect additional information, primarily by telephone, from the 61 organizations that did have strategic restructuring partnership experience, but were able to do so with only 36 (59 percent).

Findings

We found that 62 organizations, or 24 percent of the 262 organizations for which we had completed surveys, had some type of strategic restructuring experience

Table C.1
Overall Survey Yield

	Subtotals	Totals	%
Completed Surveys		262	66
▪ Strategic restructuring experience	62		
▪ No strategic restructuring experience	200		
Non-Completed Surveys		105	26
▪ Subject declined to participate	52		
▪ Incomplete surveys	53		
Deleted Cases		33	8
▪ Organization closed or moved out of city	23		
▪ Phone number could not be located	4		
▪ Phone number out of order	6		
Total	400	400	100

and 200 (76 percent) had no strategic restructuring experience. (See Tables C.1 and C.2.)

Within Cleveland, we found that 29 organizations, or 32 percent of the 91 organizations for which we had completed surveys, had some type of strategic restructuring experience and 62 (68 percent) had no strategic restructuring experience. (See Table C.3.)

Within San Francisco, we found that 33 organizations (19 percent) of the 171 organizations for which we had completed surveys had some type of strategic restructuring experience and 138 (81 percent) had no strategic restructuring experience.

For both San Francisco and Cleveland, we also determined whether there were relationships between strategic restructuring experience and three variables included in the form 990 data: total revenues, programmatic focus, and year established.[2]

Using revenue categories established in Phase I of the study, we looked at the relationship of strategic restructuring to total revenues. (See Table C.4.) Although we found a significant difference among revenue categories, the relationship between revenue and strategic restructuring experience was unclear. We then reduced the number of revenue categories from 5 to 2 and found that organizations with total revenues of more than $10 million were statistically more likely to have strategic restructuring experience than those with revenues of $200,000 to $10 million. (See Table C.5.) This result contrasts with our finding, in Phase I of the study, that, in our sample of 192 organizations, very large organizations (with budgets over $10 million) and very small organizations (with budgets less than $500,000) were less likely to be involved in strategic restructuring than were those with mid-range budgets. However, it should be noted that Phase I did not involve

Table C.2
Cleveland Survey Yield

	Subtotals	Totals	%
Completed Surveys		91	66
▪ Strategic restructuring experience	29		
▪ No strategic restructuring experience	62		
Non-Completed Surveys		37	27
▪ Subject declined to participate	23		
▪ Incomplete surveys	14		
Deleted Cases		10	7
Total	138	138	100

Table C.3
San Francisco Survey Yield

	Subtotals	Totals	%
Completed Surveys		171	65
▪ Strategic restructuring experience	33		
▪ No strategic restructuring experience	138		
Non-Completed Surveys		68	26
▪ Subject declined to participate	29		
▪ Incomplete surveys	39		
Deleted Cases		23	9
Total	262	262	100

Table C.4
Strategic Restructuring Experience by Total Revenues (using 5 revenue categories)

Total Revenues	No	Yes		Total Responses	Missing Data	Total Sample
		#	%			
$200,000 – $500,000	54	20	27	74	55	129
$500,001 – $1 M	56	7	11	63	33	96
$1,000,001 – $5 M	68	21	24	89	39	128
$5,000,001 – $10 M	12	4	25	16	6	22
> $10 M	10	10	50	20	5	25
Total	200	62	24	262	138	400

Table C.5
Strategic Restructuring Experience by Total Revenues (using 2 revenue categories)

Total Revenues	No	Yes		Total
		#	%	
$200,000 – $10 M	190	52	22	242
> $10 M	10	10	50	20
Total	200	62	24	262

$X^2 = 6.810$, df = 1, p<.01

a random sample of organizations; thus the sample in Phase II, which was randomly drawn, is probably more representative of the whole population of nonprofits that fit our parameters and probably provides a better picture of the types of nonprofits that have experienced strategic restructuring.

We found no correlation between strategic restructuring experience and either programmatic focus or year established.

Because we were able to collect additional information on only 36 of the 61 organizations that had strategic restructuring partnership experience, we could not do a statistical analysis of these data. However, we have reviewed the findings, which begin to build a picture of motivations, benefits, and other aspects of strategic restructuring according to a range of nonprofits.

Duration of Strategic Restructuring Partnerships

Among our respondents, strategic restructuring experience was most often a fairly recent experience. Twenty-six of the 36 organizations that had strategic restructuring experience had formed a partnership since 1995. Eight had not done so in this time period, and 2 did not answer this question. Nineteen had formed a partnership prior to 1995, 13 had not, 2 respondents did not know if their organization had done so, and 2 did not answer this question. Thirty-three (92 percent) respondents indicated that a strategic restructuring partnership in which their organization was involved was still functioning at the time of the survey.

Number of Organizations in a Partnership

We asked respondents to focus on one strategic restructuring partnership that their organization had engaged in, in answering the balance of the questions. The majority of these partnerships involved 2 (N = 14) or 3 (N = 7) organizations. Ten partnerships involved 4 to 6 organizations, and 5 involved more than 6.

Robustness of Typology

Based on findings from Phase I of the study, we developed the six types of strategic restructuring partnerships, which varied along four dimensions: primary purpose (administrative or programmatic), governance structure within the partnership, corporate structure changes, and degree of focus (i.e., whether the partnership was focused on a specific program, initiative, or effort, or was more broadly focused on multiple functional areas). We asked respondents to indicate if their partnerships had certain qualities related to purpose, governance, corporate structure, and degree of focus. We then analyzed responses to see if the responses clustered in the way we would predict based on the definitions of our six types of partnerships. We found that only 14 out of the 36 organizations provided responses that clustered according to our definitions. Most of the 14 fit the joint-programming category. Among those that did not fit any of the six categories, there was no clustering around any combination of dimensions. This finding may throw doubt on the typology. However, given the small size of the sample, we believe that the typology warrants further testing.

Motivations

Sixty-nine percent of the respondents indicated that an internal decision to increase the efficiency/efficacy of the organization was an important or very important motivation in forming their strategic restructuring partnerships. None of the other eight potential motivating factors was rated as important or very important by more than a third of the respondents. However, one-fourth to one-third reported that funding-related issues were a motivation. (See Table C.6.)

Benefits

Eighty-nine percent of the respondents indicated that increased services was an important or very important benefit of their strategic restructuring partnership, 83 percent indicated that increased programmatic collaboration with partner or-

Table C.6
Motivations for Forming Strategic Restructuring Partnerships

Motivating Factors	Number of respondents who indicated that the factor was important	% of total respondents
Internal decision to increase the efficiency/efficacy of the organization	25	69
Changes in funding structures (such as to managed care)	12	33
Increased competition for funding	10	28
Reduction in private funding	9	25
Pressure from funders	9	25
Reduction in public funding	5	14
Increased overhead expenses	5	14
Increased competition for clientele	5	14
Internal concern about preserving the autonomy of the organization	5	14

ganizations was an important or very important benefit, and 61 percent indicated that increased funding was an important or very important benefit. (See Table C.7.)

Reliance on Similar Funding Sources

Twenty-five respondents (69 percent) indicated that, at the time their partnerships came about, they relied on some of the same funding sources as their part-

Table C.7
Benefits of Strategic Restructuring Partnerships

Benefits	Number of respondents who indicated that the benefit was an important result of their partnership.	% of total respondents
Increased services	32	89
Increased programmatic collaboration with partner organizations	30	83
Increased funding	22	61
Increased market share/competitiveness	18	50
Increased administrative capacity/quality	17	47
Appeased funders	11	31
Preserved organizational autonomy	10	28
Reduced expenses	9	25
Prevented a reduction in size or scope of organization	5	14
Saved organization from closing	4	11

ners. Of these respondents, 8 indicated that the majority of their funders also funded their partners, 6 indicated that roughly half of their funders also funded their partners, and 10 indicated that less than half of their funders also funded their partners.

Overall Effectiveness

Seventy-two percent of respondents rated their strategic restructuring partnership as effective in meeting their organization's expectations over time.

NOTES

1. By "human services," we mean any organization that listed one of the following as their primary service area: community improvement, capacity-building; crime, legal-related; employment, job-related; food, agriculture, nutrition; housing, shelter; human services: multipurpose; mental health, crisis intervention; recreation, sports, leisure, athletics; or youth development.

2. Based on chi-square goodness-of-fit tests, we do not have reason to believe the sample is nonrepresentative in terms of: total revenues, programmatic focus, and year established.

APPENDIX D

Telephone Survey Form

Organization Name: _____

Name & Phone of Person Completing Survey:_____

STRATEGIC RESTRUCTURING

NONPROFIT SURVEY

1a. Has your organization ever partnered with one or more other organizations to either increase administrative efficiency or further the programmatic mission of the organizations?

❑ YES

❑ NO   If you answered NO, you have finished the survey. Thank you.

1b. (If Yes) Have any of these partnerships involved the sharing, transferring, or consolidation of services, resources, or programs?

❑ YES

❑ NO   If you answered NO, you have finished the survey. Thank you.

If you answered YES to question 1a and b, please complete questions 2a and 2b below.

2a. Have any of YOUR organization s partnerships with OTHER organizations included: A commitment among the organizations to continue for the foreseeable future (rather than being a time-limited project)?

❑ YES

❑ NO

Shared or transferred decision-making power over program or administrative functions among the organizations involved?

❏ YES

❏ NO

Some sort of formal agreement among the organizations involved?

❏ YES

❏ NO

2b.   Please answer true or false: The **ONLY** types of partnerships my organization has participated in have been partnerships limited to: sharing information, coordinating programs, or conducting joint planning.

❏ True

❏ False

THANK YOU FOR PARTICIPATING! WE MAY CONTACT YOU TO FOLLOW UP ON THE INFORMATION YOU HAVE PROVIDED.

APPENDIX E

Study Participants

CASE STUDY INTERVIEWEES

John Begley
Executive Director
Louisville Visual Art Association

Ashley Belden
Neighborhood Outreach Specialist
STEPS at Liberty Center, Inc.

Larry Brenner
Former Staff Member
ACHIEVE

Tammy J. Brooks
The SUMMIT Therapy Center

Brion Clinkingbeard
Curator/Director of Exhibitions
Kentucky Art and Craft Foundation, Inc.

Deirdre Cochran
Former Executive Director
Zonta Services

Allan Cowen
President and CEO
Fund for the Arts

Lillian Cruz
Executive Director
Humanidad Incorporated

Bobbi Douglas
Executive Director
STEPS at Liberty Center, Inc., and Every Woman's House, Inc.

Tom Dreschler
School Director
ACHIEVE

David Eve
Vice President, Information and Technology
Partners for Community

Heriberto Flores
Chairman
Partners for Community

Holly French
Finance Director
Kentucky Art and Craft Foundation, Inc.

David Gadaire
Executive Director
CareerPoint

Patricia Gardner
Former Staff Member
ACHIEVE

Lara Ginsburg
Operations Director
STEPS at Liberty Center, Inc.

Jeannette Glasser
Clinical Director
ACHIEVE

Jeffrey Greim
Chief Operating Officer
Partners for Community

Robert W. Griffith
Attorney
Stites & Harbison

Paul A. Guggenheim
Executive Director
Core Behavioral Health Centers

Mac Hawkins
Finance Director
Every Woman's House, Inc.

Ronald E. Holtman
Attorney
Logee, Hostetler, Stutzman, & Lehman

Kathy Kalm
Teacher
ACHIEVE

Tom Kilcoyne
Cohen, Todd, Kite, and Stanford, LLC

David C. Knopf
Business Manager
J. B. Speed Art Museum

John W. Kropf
Attorney
Kropf, Wagner, & Hohenberger

Robert T. Lameier
President
Miami Savings Bank

Ray Lancaster
Microenterprise Specialist
Spokane Neighborhood Action Programs

Lou Lesher
Manager
TriArt Gallery

Leland Levy
Board Member
ACHIEVE

Brenda P. Linnick
Executive Director
United Way of Wayne & Holmes Counties, Inc.

Carmen Luz
Program Director
New England Farm Workers' Council

Pam McClain
Vice President
Talbert House, Inc.

Clyde Miller
Manager, 281-CARE
Talbert House, Inc.

Mary Miller
Executive Director
Kentucky Art and Craft Foundation, Inc.

Lorraine Montalto
Program Director
Corporation for Public Management

Peter Morrin
Director
J. B. Speed Art Museum

Sharon Nissley
Domestic Violence Advocate
Every Woman's House, Inc.

Michael P. Oberdoerster
Medical Director
Core Behavioral Health Centers

Anne Ogden
Administrative Director
J. B. Speed Art Museum

Jim Patterson
Former Board Member
ACHIEVE

Russell Peguero-Winters
Director of Case Management
Core Behavioral Health Centers

Bill Persch
Director, Marketing
Partners for Community

Philip Pinsukanjana
Former Staff Member
ACHIEVE

Marjorie Pitterman
Board Member
Louisville Visual Art Association

Carol Pliner
Board Member
ACHIEVE

Carla Preston
Business Development Specialist
Small Business Development Center

Magaly Ramos-Cartagena
School Director
ACHIEVE

Stuart Schloss
Ulmer and Berne, LLP

Allen Schmelzer
CCIM
Community Development, City of Spokane

Stephen Shapiro
Board Member
STEPS at Liberty Center, Inc.

Roger Smith
Clinical Director
Core Behavioral Health Centers

Jean Spurr
Director of Human Resources
ACHIEVE

Rita Steinberg
Director of Corporate Giving
Indianapolis Symphony Orchestra

Larry Stuckart
Executive Director
Spokane Neighborhood Action Programs

Gail Switzer
Executive Director
ACHIEVE

Neil Tilow
President and CEO
Talbert House, Inc.

Patrick Tribbe
President/CEO
Hamilton County Community Mental Health Board

Renee Warner
Business Development Officer
Northwest Business Development Association

Jerome L. Weiner
President
Corporation for Public Management

Patrick Welsh
Board Member
Kentucky Art and Craft Foundation, Inc.

Gary Whelpley
President
Northwest Business Development Association

Lisa Work
Associate Director
Louisville Visual Art Association

Beverly Zemrock
Social Services
Wooster Community Hospital

NONPROFIT AND PHILANTHROPIC LEADER INTERVIEWEES

Alan J. Abramson
Director
Nonprofit Sector Research Fund

Audrey R. Alvarado
Executive Director
National Council of Nonprofit Associations

Elizabeth T. Boris
Center Director
Center on Nonprofits and Philanthropy, The Urban Institute

Jeffrey L. Bradach
Cofounder and Managing Partner
The Bridgespan Group

Peter C. Brinckerhoff
Corporate Alternatives, Inc.

James V. Denova
Senior Program Officer
Claude Worthington Benedum Foundation

Sara L. Engelhardt
President
The Foundation Center

Virginia Hodgkinson
Center for the Study of Voluntary Organizations and Public Service
Georgetown Public Policy Institute

MaryAnn Holohean
Program Director
The Meyer Foundation

Barbara Kibbe
Program Officer
David and Lucile Packard Foundation

Christine Letts
Lecturer in Public Policy; Associate Director
Hauser Center for Nonprofit Institutions
Harvard University

Jan Masaoka
Executive Director
CompassPoint Nonprofit Services

Sara E. Meléndez
President
Independent Sector

Dorothy S. Ridings
President and CEO
Council on Foundations

Mark Rosenman
Vice President
The Union Institute, Office for Social Responsibility

William Ryan
Research Fellow
Hauser Center for Nonprofit Institutions
Harvard University

Lester Salamon
Professor
Institute for Policy Studies, Johns Hopkins University

Benjamin Shute
Secretary and Treasurer
Rockefeller Brothers Fund

Elizabeth Skidmore
Division Director, National Center for Consultation and Professional
    Development
Child Welfare League of America

Eugene R. Tempel
Executive Director
Center on Philanthropy at Indiana University

APPENDIX F

Case Study Partnerships

Joint Programming:
Spokane County Microenterprise Development Program

Northwest Business Development Association
Makes loans to small businesses
Gary Whelpley, President

Spokane Neighborhood Action Program
Provides human services
Larry Stuckart, Executive Director

Administrative Consolidation:
The STEPS–Every Woman's House Case

Every Woman's House, Inc.
Provides shelter and services for abused women
Bobbi Douglas, Executive Director

STEPS (Substance Abuse, Treatment, Education, and Prevention Services)
    at Liberty Center, Inc.
Bobbi Douglas, Executive Director

Management Service Organization: Partners for Community

Corporation for Public Management
Provides human services
Jerome L. Weiner, President

New England Farm Workers' Council
Provides human services
Heriberto Flores, Executive Director

Joint Venture: TriArt Gallery and Gift Shop

Kentucky Art and Craft Foundation
Visual arts organization
Mary Miller, Executive Director

Louisville Visual Art Association
Visual arts organization
John Begley, Executive Director

J. B. Speed Art Museum
Visual arts organization
Peter Morrin, Director

Parent-Subsidiary: Talbert House–Core Case

Core Behavioral Health Care
Provides mental health services
Paul A. Guggenheim, Executive Director

Talbert House
Provides human services
Neil Tilow, President and CEO

Merger: ACHIEVE

Peninsula Children's Center
Provided services to children with physical and mental disabilities
Gail Switzer, Former Executive Director

Zonta Services
Provided services to children with physical and mental disabilities
Deirdre Cochran, Former Executive Director

Bibliography

(1999). *State mental health agency profiling system*. The National Association of State Mental Health Program Directors Research Institute, Inc. <nri.rdmc.org> (accessed 2001).

(2001). *The nonprofit almanac*. Washington, DC: The Independent Sector, 3.

Abzug, R., & Green, S. (1999). *Executive concerns: Issues on the minds of New York City nonprofit CEOs and CFOs*. New York: New School University, 32.

Anonymous. (January 4, 1997). Why too many mergers miss the mark. *The Economist*.

Campbell, D. A. (2000). *Interorganizational restructuring in nonprofit human service agencies*. Cleveland, OH: Mandel School of Applied Social Sciences, Case Western Reserve University, 300.

Cartwright, S., & Cooper, C. L. (1996). *Managing merger, acquisitions, and strategic alliances: Integrating people and cultures*. Oxford: Butterworth-Heinemann.

Cowin, K., & Moore, G. (1996). Critical success factors for merger in the UK voluntary sector. *Voluntas*, 7 (March), 66–86.

Creed, W. E. D., & R. Miles (1996). A conceptual framework linking organizational forms, managerial philosophies, and the opportunity costs of controls. In R. M. Kramer and T. R. Tyler (Eds.), *Trust in organizations: Frontiers of theory and research*. Thousand Oaks, CA: Sage Publications, ix, 429.

DiMaggio, P. J., & W. W. Powell (1983). The iron cage revisited: institutional isomorphism and collective rationality in organizational fields. *American Sociological Review*, 48 (April), 147–160.

Foster-Fishman, P. G., Salem, D. A., Allen, N. E., & Fahrbach, K. (1999). Ecological factors impacting provider attitudes toward human service delivery reform. *American Journal of Community Psychology*, 27 (6), 785–816.

Galaskiewicz, J., & Bielefeld, W. (1998). *Nonprofit organizations in an age of uncertainty*. New York: Aldine De Gruyter.

Goldman, S., & Kahnweiler, W. M. (2000). A collaborator profile for executives of nonprofit organizations. *Nonprofit Management & Leadership*, 10 (4), 435–450.

Golensky, M., & DeRuiter, G. L. (1999). *The urge to merge: Lessons from the nonprofit sector*. Paper presented at the annual conference of the Association for Research on Nonprofit Organizations and Voluntary Action (ARNOVA), Arlington, VA.

Grønbjerg, K. A. (1993). *Understanding nonprofit funding: Managing revenues in social services and community development organizations*. San Francisco: Jossey-Bass.

Hannan, M. T., & Freeman, J. (1984). Structural inertia and organizational change. *American Sociological Review*, 49 (April), 149–164.

Harris, M., Harris, J., Hutchison, R., & Rochester, C. (1999). Mergers, collaborations, and alliances: Drivers of change in the UK voluntary sector. Birmingham, England: Aston Business School.

Heath, S. B., & McLaughlin, M. W. (1993). *Identity and inner-city youth: Beyond ethnicity and gender*. New York: Teachers College Press.

Hubbard, N. (1999). *Acquisition strategy and implementation*. Houndmills, Basingstoke, Hampshire [England]: Macmillan.

Johnston, D. C. (2000). Creating waves in nonprofit sea: Bain & Co. comes up with an entirely new thing. *The New York Times*. 2 February 2000, C1 & C12.

Kalleberg, A. L., & Van Buren, M. E. (1996). Is bigger better? Explaining the relationship between organization size and job rewards. *American Sociological Review*, 61 (February), 47–66.

Kohm, A., La Piana, D., Gowdy, H. (2000). *Strategic restructuring: Findings from a study of integrations and alliances among nonprofit social service and cultural organizations in the United States*. Chicago: Chapin Hall Center for Children, 54.

Kushner, R. J. (1997). *Contrasting theory and promise with practice and performance: Network formation in community nonprofit organizations*. Paper presented at the annual conference of the Association for Research on Nonprofit Organizations and Voluntary Action (ARNOVA), New York, NY.

La Piana, D. (1997). *Beyond collaboration: Strategic restructuring of nonprofit organizations*. San Francisco: The James Irvine Foundation.

Lajoux, A. R., & Weston, J. F. (1998). Do deals deliver on postmerger performance? *Mergers and Acquisitions*, 33 (2), 34–37.

Light, P. C. (2000). *Making nonprofits work: A report on the tides of nonprofit management reform*. Washington, DC: Brookings Institution Press.

McMurtry, S. L., Netting, F. E., & Kettner, P. M. (1991). How nonprofits adapt to a stringent environment. *Nonprofit Management & Leadership*, I (3), 235–252.

Meier, J. (1997). Strategic alliance fund, evaluation 1996–97. New York: Arete Corporation.

Mishra, A. K. (1996). Organizational response to crisis: The centrality of trust. In R. M. Kramer and T. R. Tyler (Eds.), *Trust in organizations: Frontiers of theory and research*. Thousand Oaks, CA: Sage Publications, ix, 429.

Peters, J., & Wolfred, T. (2001). Daring to lead: Nonprofit executive directors and their work experience. San Francisco: CompassPoint Nonprofit Services, 46.

Powell, W. W. (1996). Trust-based forms of governance. In R. M. Kramer and T. R. Tyler (Eds.), *Trust in organizations: Frontiers of theory and research*. Thousand Oaks, CA: Sage Publications, ix, 429.

Provan, K. G., Milward, H. B., & Isett, K. R. (2001). *Collaboration and integration of community-based health and human services in a nonprofit managed care system.* Washington DC: Nonprofit Sector Research Fund Working Paper Series, 22.

Reisch, M., & Sommerfeld, D. (2000). *Welfare reform and the transformation of nonprofit organizations.* Paper presented at the Annual Conference of the Association for Research on Nonprofit Organizations and Voluntary Action, New Orleans, LA.

Reisch, M., & Sommerfeld, D. (2001). *Assessing the impact of welfare reform on nonprofit organizations in southeast Michigan: Implications for policy and practice.* Washington, DC: Nonprofit Sector Research Fund, The Aspen Institute, 64.

Reitan, T. C. (1998). Theories of interorganizational relations in the human services. *Social Service Review,* September, 285–309.

Salamon, L. M. (1997). *Private action/public good: Maryland's nonprofit sector in a time of change.* Baltimore, MD: Maryland Association of Nonprofit Organizations: 67–68.

Scheff, J., & Kotler, P. (1996). How the arts can prosper through strategic collaborations. *Harvard Business Review,* January, 52.

Schmid, H. (1992). Executive leadership in human service organizations. In Y. Hasenfeld (Ed.), *Human services as complex organizations.* Newbury Park, CA: Sage Publications, 98–117.

Singer, M. I., & Yankey, J. A. (summer 1991). Organizational metamorphosis: A study of eighteen nonprofit mergers, acquisitions, and consolidations. *Nonprofit Management & Leadership,* 1, 357–369.

Tucker, D. J., Baum, & J. A., Singh, J. V. (1992). The institutional ecology of human service organizations. In Y. Hasenfeld (Ed.), *Human services as complex organizations.* Newbury Park, CA: Sage Publications, 47–72.

Tuite, M. F. (1972). Interorganizational decision making—A multidisciplinary perspective. In M. Tuite, R. K. Chisholm, and M. Radnor (Eds.), *Interorganizational decision making.* Chicago: Aldine Pub. Co., xvi, 298.

Twombly, E. C. (2000). *Assessing the Adaptive Responses of Human Service Nonprofits in Devolving Social Service Systems.* Paper presented at the Annual Conference of the Association for Research on Nonprofit Organizations and Voluntary Action, New Orleans, LA.

Warren, R. L. (1972). The concerting of decisions as a variable in organizational interaction. In M. Tuite, R. K. Chisholm, and M. Radnor (Eds.), *Interorganizational decision making.* Chicago: Aldine Pub. Co., xvi, 298.

Wernet, S. P. (1999). *Managed care in human services.* Chicago, IL: Lyceum Books.

Williams, L. L. (2000). *Strategic alliance decisions: The interpersonal experience of alliance building.* Paper presented at the Conference of the Association for Research on Nonprofit Organizations and Voluntary Action, New Orleans, LA.

Wulczyn, F., & Orlebeke, B. (2000). Fiscal reform and managed care in child welfare services. *Policy & Practice of Public Human Services,* 58 (3), 26–31.

Yankey, J. A., Wester, B., Koney, K. M., & McClellan, A. (1999). *Nonprofit leadership roundtable on the similarities and differences between nonprofit and for-profit strategic alliances.* Medina, OH: Mandel Center for Nonprofit Organizations, Case Western Reserve University.

Index

ACHIEVE, 8, 24–25; case study, 111–17; communication issues, 57; financial impacts, 33; morale and leadership problems, 43, 44–45, 46, 48, 58, 115–16; motives for restructuring, 113; name change, 50; organizational cultural differences, 47–49, 57, 115, 116; restructuring planning and implementation, 55–56, 114–15; services impacts, 114, 116; staff benefits improvement, 35; staff characteristics, 59–60; staff reductions, 32, 52; staff sharing, 35, 114, 115

Administrative consolidation, 6, 73; benefits and challenges, 70–71 table; case study, 83–90. *See also* STEPS–Every Woman's House partnership

Administrative costs, 31–32, 33; ratio to program expenses, 15

Administrative efficiency, 11–12

Alliances, 5, 6–7

Alvarado, Audrey R., 64, 66

Arts organizations, 12

Asselin, Jim, 92, 95

Assessment: programs and efficiency, 2, 12–13, 26, 27–28; restructuring results, 32, 34

Begley, John, 99, 100, 101, 102

Benefits of restructuring, 31–38, 70 table, 72

Bielefeld, Wolfgang, 14

Block grants, 2

Board members, post-restructuring issues, 42–43, 50–51

Boris, Elizabeth, 62–63, 64

Bradach, Jeffrey, 20, 63, 64–65, 67

Brand loyalty, 49–50

Brightwood Development Corporation, 93

Brinckerhoff, Peter C., 67

Brooks, Tammy, 85, 86

Campbell, David, 58, 59

Capacity building, 67

CareerPoint, 93, 95

Cartwright, Sue, 42, 46

Case studies, 79–117; about, 8–9; ACHIEVE, 111–17; interviewees listed, 133–38; methodology, 120; Partners for Community, 90–97;

Case Studies (*continued*)
  research recommendations, 76;
  Spokane County Microenterprise
  Development Program, 79–83;
  STEPS–Every Woman's House
  partnership, 83–90; Talbert
  House–Core partnership, 103–11;
  TriArt partnership, 97–103
Challenges. *See* Costs and challenges
  of restructuring
Client services. *See* Program *entries*;
  Services
Client tracking, 2, 95
Clinkingbeard, Brion, 41, 43, 101
Cochran, Deirdre, 113, 114, 115
Collaboration, 6; barriers to, 19
Commercialization, concerns about, 67
Community Crossroads, 87
Competition, 2, 3, 11–13, 61–63, 67
Consultants, 73–74
Contract failure, 1, 12, 16 n. 2
Cooper, Cary L., 42, 46
Core Behavioral Health Care, 103. *See
  also* Talbert House–Core Behavioral
  Health Care partnership
Corporate mergers, 3, 40, 41, 42
Corporation for Public Management
  (CPM), 7, 90. *See also* Partners for
  Community
Corporations, for-profit. *See* For-profit
  organizations
Cost-benefit analysis, 41–42; research
  recommendations, 75–76
Cost efficiency: alternative strategies,
  26; as restructuring motive, 26, 63
Costs and challenges of restructuring,
  39–53, 71 table, 72–75; financial
  costs, 33, 41–42, 73–74; identity
  issues, 49–51; morale and
  leadership problems, 42–46, 57–58,
  72–73; organizational cultural
  differences, 40–41, 46–49; staff
  turnover, 33, 51–52; time costs,
  39–41, 43, 44
Cost savings benefits, 31–33, 72
Cowen, Allan, 44, 100, 101, 102
Cowin, Kate, 57

CPM. *See* Corporation for Public
  Management
Creed, Douglas, 58
Cruz, Lillian, 37, 50, 95, 97
Cultural differences between
  organizations, 40–41, 46–49, 51

Database sharing, 35
Decision making: cultural differences,
  47; information access/
  communications and, 45–46, 57, 60;
  organization size and, 66; time
  costs of, 40, 44
Demographic changes, 64
Denova, James, 62, 64
DeRuiter, Gerald L., 42, 52
DiMaggio, Paul, 14, 28, 63
Douglas, Bobbi, 33, 85, 86–87, 88, 89

Efficiency, 11–12; as concern of
  funders, 14, 23–24; difficulty of
  assessing, 12–13, 26, 27–28;
  potential impacts of efficiency
  focus, 26; as restructuring motive,
  26
Employees. *See* Executive directors;
  Staff *entries*
Engelhardt, Sara, 62
Eve, David, 45
Every Woman's House, 83. *See also*
  STEPS–Every Woman's House
  partnership
Executive directors: as champions of
  restructuring, 59, 60; experienced,
  shortage of, 2, 27, 37; fundraising
  and, 27; organizational reputation
  and, 37; post-restructuring
  problems and challenges, 43, 44–45;
  sharing, 27, 37; survey of, 2, 27;
  turnover challenges, 52
Expertise sharing, as restructuring
  benefit, 34–35, 72

Facility sharing, 87–88. *See also* TriArt
  partnership
Faith-based human service
  organizations, 62, 64

Financial concerns: financial costs of restructuring, 33, 41–42, 73–74; as restructuring motive, 23–26, 65–66. *See also* Cost *entries*; Funding

Flores, Heriberto, 29, 45, 58, 91–92, 93, 95, 96, 97

For-profit organizations: competition from, 2, 62; corporate mergers, 3, 40, 41, 42

Foster-Fishman, Pennie G., 19, 59

Freeman, John, 48, 55

Fund for the Arts, 24, 44, 99–100

Funding: competition for, 2, 14–15, 62; funders' expectations and perceptions, 2, 14, 23–24, 63, 65, 72; government funders, 2, 62; increased, as strategic restructuring benefit, 33; leaders' relations with funders, 27, 45; maintenance of, as restructuring motive, 23–25, 29 n. 1, 62, 65–66; organization size and, 65, 67

Gadaire, David, 36–37, 95

Galaskiewicz, Joseph, 14

Gardner, Patricia, 47–48, 116

Gault, Stanley, 86

Ginsburg, Lara, 45, 89

Goldman, Samuel, 59

Golensky, Martha, 42, 52

Government funders, 2, 62

Greim, Jeff, 93, 96

Griffith, Robert W., 24, 100–101

Grønbjerg, Kirsten, 16 n. 2, 19

Guggenheim, Paul, 44, 50, 105, 110; on organizational identity, 108; restructuring planning and implementation, 106, 107; on Talbert-Core's future, 111

Hamilton County Community Mental Health Board, 24

Hannan, Michael, 48, 55

Harris, Margaret, 24, 51

Hawkins, Mac, 89

Heath, Shirley Brice, 50

Hodgkinson, Virginia, 67

Holtman, Ron, 50–51

Humanidad Incorporated, 37, 50, 93–94, 95

Human service organizations, 11, 13; demographic changes and, 64; faith-based, 62, 64; managed care and, 2, 13, 24–25, 62; vouchers for services, 61–62

Identity, post-restructuring issues, 49–51

Implementation planning, 75

Information access, decision making and, 45–46, 57, 60

Information sharing, 34–35, 40, 73

Innovation, restructuring and, 66

Integrations, 5, 7–8, 20

International Language Institute of Massachusetts, 93

Interviews. *See* Leader interviews

Isomorphism, 14, 28

Joint programming, 6, 20, 56, 69, 73; benefits and challenges, 70–71 table; case study, 79–83. *See also* Spokane County Microenterprise Development Program

Joint ventures, 7; benefits and challenges, 70–71 table; case study, 97–103; consultants for, 73–74. *See also* TriArt partnership

KACF. *See* Kentucky Art and Craft Foundation

Kahnweiler, William, 59

Kalleberg, Arne, 36

Kentucky Art and Craft Foundation (KACF), 7, 41, 44, 97. *See also* TriArt partnership

Kibbe, Barbara, 64, 67

Kilcoyne, Tom, 111

Kropf, John, 86

Kushner, Roland, 45

Lajoux, A. R., 41

Lameier, Robert T., 49–50, 105

Lancaster, Ray, 57, 81, 82, 83

Layoffs. *See* Staff reduction

Leader interviews, 20–21;
    interviewees listed, 138–39;
    methodology, 121; predictions
    about future restructuring trends,
    61–68; research recommendations,
    75–77
Leadership: experienced, shortage of,
    2, 27, 37, 64; future leaders, 64;
    post-restructuring problems and
    challenges, 43–46, 48, 57–58, 72–73;
    sharing of, 27, 37, 43–44. *See also*
    Executive directors; Staff *entries*
Letts, Christine, 65, 67
Light, Paul, 26, 34
Louisville Visual Art Association
    (LVAA), 7, 97. *See also* TriArt
    partnership

Malone, Jane, 93
Managed care, 2, 9 n.3, 13, 24–25, 62
Managed Care in Human Services
    (Wernet), 13
Management: perceived legitimacy
    and, 14, 32–33, 63, 72; public and
    funder expectations about, 14, 15,
    23–24, 32–33
Management service organizations
    (MSOs), 7, 25; benefits and
    challenges, 70–71 table; case study,
    90–97. *See also* Partners for
    Community
Maryland nonprofits surveys, 17, 18,
    21 n. 1
McClain, Pam, 60, 110
McLaughlin, Milbrey, 50
Meier, James, 33
Mercer Management Consulting
    corporate merger study, 40
Mergers, corporate, 3, 40, 41, 42
Mergers, nonprofit, 7, 57; benefits and
    challenges, 70–71 table; case study,
    111–17; consultants for, 73–74;
    morale problems, 42; motives for,
    26. *See also* ACHIEVE
Miles, Raymond, 58
Miller, Mary, 44, 102–3
Mishra, Aneil K., 58
Moore, Geoff, 57
Morale problems, 42–43

Morrin, Peter, 99, 101, 102
Motives for restructuring, 14, 23–29,
    69–70
MSOs. *See* Management service
    organizations

Name changes, 50
New England Farm Workers'
    Council, 7, 29, 90. *See also* Partners
    for Community
Niche nonprofits, 64–65, 66–67
Nonprofit sector: changes and
    responses to change, 1–3;
    competition in, 2, 3, 11–13, 61–63,
    67; homogenization in, 14;
    potential impacts of efficiency
    focus, 26; potential impacts of
    restructuring, 66–68; researching
    impacts on, 76; strategic
    restructuring trend, 61–66
Northwest Business Development
    Association, 6, 28, 34, 52, 80. *See
    also* Spokane County
    Microenterprise Development
    Program

Oberdoerster, Michael, 58, 105, 110
Organizational anorexia, 15, 16 n. 1
Organizational culture differences,
    40–41, 46–49, 51
Organizational identity, post-
    restructuring issues, 49–51
Organizational size: managed care
    and, 25; restructuring impacts on
    small nonprofits, 64–65, 66–67;
    restructuring rates and, 18, 19–20,
    21 n. 1, 55; staff pay and benefits
    and, 36
Orlebeke, Britany, 25

Parent-subsidiary partnerships, 7, 74;
    case study, 103–11; example, 7–8.
    See also Talbert House–Core
    Behavioral Health Care partnership
Partners for Community (PfC), 25, 27;
    affiliates, 93–94; case study, 90–97;
    cost savings, 31–32, 95; leadership
    challenges, 45–46; organizational

cultural differences, 47, 49, 95, 96; organizational identity issues, 50, 95; reputation enhancement, 36–37; restructuring planning and implementation, 56, 57, 58, 92–93, 96; services impacts, 34, 95; staff benefits improvement, 35, 95; staff reductions and turnover, 51, 52, 95; staff sharing, 34

Partnership lifecycles, research recommendations, 76

Partnership types, 4–8; partnership matrix, 5 fig. *See also specific types*

Peguero-Winters, Russell, 59

Peninsula Children's Center, 8, 35, 46, 112. *See also* ACHIEVE

Persch, Bill, 36, 47

PfC. *See* Partners for Community

Planning for restructuring, 55–56, 72–74, 75

Powell, Walter, 14, 28, 58, 63

Prevalence of restructuring: current, 17–21; future trends, 61–66; survey findings, 19–21, 124–30; survey methodology, 120, 123–24

Program choice, cost efficiency and, 26

Program evaluation, 2, 13, 28. *See also* Assessment

Program expenses, ratio to administrative expenses, 15

Program sharing: benefits and challenges, 70–71 table. *See also* Joint programming; Joint ventures; Mergers, nonprofit; Parent-subsidiary partnerships

Program tracking systems, sharing, 33, 35, 94–95

Provan, Keith, 25

Public policy changes, competition and, 2, 61–62

Public relations, 72, 75. *See also* Reputation

Quality indicators, lack of, 12–13, 26, 27–28

Ramos-Cartagena, Magaly, 114

Reputation: enhancement, as restructuring benefit, 36–38, 72; enhancement, as restructuring motive, 27–29; identity issues after restructuring, 49–51; management and, 14, 15, 23–24, 32–33. *See also* Public relations

Research methodology, 19, 119–21, 123–24

Research recommendations, 75–77

Resource dependency theory, 13–14

Ridings, Dorothy S., 62

Rosenman, Mark, 61–62, 64, 66, 67

Ryan, William, 65

SAF (Strategic Alliance Fund), 33

Salamon, Lester, 20–21, 62–63, 67

Schloss, Stuart, 106, 107

Schmid, Hillel, 19

Services: duplication of, 11–12, 67; fees for, 3, 16 n. 2; improvements as restructuring benefit, 34; supply and demand, 12; vouchers for, 61–62

Shapiro, Steve, 89

Shute, Benjamin, 20, 66, 67

Singer, Mark, 26

Size of organization. *See* Organizational size

Skidmore, Elizabeth, 63–64, 66

SNAP. *See* Spokane Neighborhood Action Program

Speed Art Museum, 7, 24, 28–29, 97. *See also* TriArt partnership

Spokane County Microenterprise Development Program, 6, 28; case study, 79–83; financial costs, 42, 82; pre-restructuring planning, 56; services improvements, 34; staff sharing, 34; staff turnover challenges, 52; time costs, 82

Spokane Neighborhood Action Program (SNAP), 6, 28, 34, 52, 80. *See also* Spokane County Microenterprise Development Program

Spurr, Jean, 44, 114

Staff benefits improvement, 35–36, 37–38

Staff expectations, 74–75
Staff loyalty, organizational identity
    and, 50
Staff morale problems, 42–43
Staff reduction, 51–52; cost savings
    from, 31–32
Staff resources, competition for, 63–64
Staff sharing: benefits of, 34–35; cost
    savings from, 31, 32; as
    restructuring motive, 27, 64
Staff support, as success factor, 56, 72
Staff turnover, 33, 51–52
Steinberg, Rita, 99, 100, 101, 102
STEPS, 6, 83
STEPS–Every Woman's House
    partnership, 6–7, 25, 27, 28, 45; case
    study, 83–90; financial impacts, 31,
    33, 42, 88; organizational identity
    issues, 50–51; public relations
    benefits, 36, 88; shared facility
    management, 87–88; staff sharing,
    35, 87, 88, 89; staff turnover
    challenges, 52, 86–87
Strategic Alliance Fund (SAF), 33
Strategic restructuring: assessment of,
    32, 34; barriers to, 19; benefits of,
    31–38, 70 table, 72; vs. corporate
    mergers, 3, 40, 41, 42; cost-benefit
    analysis of, 41–42, 75–76; costs and
    challenges of, 39–53, 71 table,
    72–75; current prevalence of, 17–21;
    defined, 3; fundamental questions,
    8, 11–17; funder perspectives,
    23–24, 63, 65, 76–77; motives for,
    14, 23–29, 69–70; partnership types,
    4–8; potential impacts on nonprofit
    sector, 66–68; prevalence survey
    findings, 19–21, 124–30; prevalence
    trends, 61–66; research
    recommendations, 75–77; success
    factors, 55–60, 74–75. See also
    specific types
Strategic Solutions, 18
Stuckart, Larry, 81, 82–83
Success factors, 55–60, 74–75
Supply and demand, 13
Survey methodology, 19, 119–21,
    123–24

Switzer, Gail, 113, 117; on
    organizational cultural differences,
    47–48, 49, 57; post-restructuring
    staff problems, 44–45, 46, 48, 58,
    115–16; restructuring planning and
    implementation, 114–15

Talbert House, 1–2, 3, 26, 44, 103
Talbert House–Core Behavioral
    Health Care partnership, 7–8, 24;
    case study, 103–11; cost savings, 31,
    32, 109; growth of trust in, 59;
    leadership problems and
    challenges, 44, 45, 58, 108, 110;
    motives for restructuring, 104–6;
    organizational cultural differences,
    47, 48, 107, 109; organizational
    identity issues, 49–50, 106, 108,
    109–10; restructuring planning and
    implementation, 55, 106–8; services
    improvements, 34, 108; staff
    benefits improvement, 35–36, 108;
    staff improvements, 108–9; staff
    reductions and turnover, 52, 108;
    staff sharing, 34, 35; time costs,
    40, 109
Technology: expertise sharing and,
    35; shared, 94–95
Telephone survey form, 131–32
Tilow, Neil: leadership challenges, 45;
    on organizational identity issues,
    50; on partners' roles, 44, 110; on
    program cost efficiency, 26;
    restructuring planning and
    implementation, 40, 106, 107; on
    Talbert-Core's future, 111
Time costs of restructuring, 39–41,
    43, 44
TriArt partnership, 28–29; case study,
    97–103; dissolution of, 102;
    financial impacts, 42, 100, 102;
    morale and leadership problems,
    43, 44, 100–101; public relations
    problems, 37, 101; restructuring
    planning and implementation,
    55–56, 99–100; staff characteristics

and, 59–60; staff turnover
  challenges, 52, 102; time costs, 40,
  41, 43, 101
Tribbe, Patrick, 24, 50, 104–5
Trust, 46, 58–59, 72, 74
Tucker, David J., 36
Twombly, E. C., 55

Underserved communities, potential
  restructuring impacts, 66–67
Unnecessary replication, 11, 67

Van Buren, Mark, 36
Venture philanthropy, 63
Volume buying, 31
Vouchers, 61–62

Warren, Roland, 23
Wayne County Alcoholism Services.
  See STEPS; STEPS–Every Woman's
  House partnership

Weiner, Jerome: on benefits of
  restructuring, 94; on future of PfC,
  97; leadership sharing, 45, 92–93;
  motives for restructuring, 91, 92;
  on organizational cultural
  differences, 49; restructuring
  planning and implementation, 56,
  57, 58, 92–93, 96; on staff buy-in,
  96; on staff reductions/changes,
  31–32, 51
Wernet, Stephen, 13, 25
Weston, J. Fred, 41
Whelpley, Gary, 82
Williams, Lauren, 58, 59
Wulcyzn, Fred, 25

Yankey, John, 26, 32

Zemrock, Beverly, 86
Zonta Services, 8, 35, 46, 112. See also
  ACHIEVE

About the Authors

AMELIA KOHM is a Researcher at the Chapin Hall Center for Children at the University of Chicago.

DAVID LA PIANA is a Founder of La Piana Associates, Inc., a consulting firm specializing in strategic solutions for nonprofit organizations and foundations.